LIFE, LOVE AND WAR

Life, Love and War by John Windhorst

Edited by Robyn Holleran

Books may be purchased by contacting the publisher and author at:

ISBN: 9781695142053

First Edition

Printed by Kindle direct publishing, An Amazon.com Company

Authors note: The names written may not be transcribed with the correct spelling.

For

Dave and Gayle, Dan and Denise, Pete, Kelly, Johnny, Chris, Tammy, Sarah, Matt, Ben & Robby

Preface

My grandmother was Arlene Reuter Windhorst. Growing up, I often heard "Grandma was a nurse in WWII," and every so often I'd ask her about this; however, I never really knew the right questions to ask about her service. She was a fun grandma and we just enjoyed her for who she was when we knew her.

Unfortunately, as more questions came to mind once I got older, her memory was giving away to dementia and finally Alzheimer's, the disease that took untold recollections, and her life, away from us. Right before she passed away in 2007, Grandma left me her diary from when she served in World War II, something she knew I would be interested in, partly as an avid collector and WWII history buff.

Oddly enough, I had it locked away in a safe for many years after her passing before I opened it. Why? I liked not knowing what was in there—that it could be anything. That it was solely HERS.

When I cracked it open, I was immediately reminded of how bad her handwriting was! But as I began to peruse and decipher what she had written, a whole new and amazing picture of who my grandmother was began to emerge...

Her involvement in the war was truly a calling. Hearing stories from family involved in WWI inspired her to pursue a nursing career. After Pearl Harbor, she jumped to enlist, like so many did. In particular, the song, "Rose of No Man's Land," about the famous nurse Florence Nightingale that enthralled her as a small child, meant something else now as a young adult and fueled her decision.

She entered the Army and, after basic training, was assigned to the Third General Hospital, Mt. Sinai, N.Y. unit and was aboard the French ship Louis Pasteur on a long voyage to Casablanca. Just the START of a war-long trip that would have momentous stops.

Stationed in a tent hospital on the northeast coast of Africa, she got her first taste of wartime treatment, serving veterans of the war in Italy. The experience horrified and numbed her, but she credits the courageous, and even good natured soldiers for getting her through the initial shocks.

Her next adventure began aboard the famous Queen Mary, which transported her along the first stage in a long journey that landed near Omaha Beach. There, she saw firsthand the scenery from the stories she had heard about the hellish, unsheltered landing of Allied soldiers and their struggle against enemy forces. This experience stayed with her forever.

The trip ended in France at what eventually became a prisoner of war hospital. The bloody horrors of war that soldiers saw, that she now witnessed firsthand and was required to treat, were not the only atrocites; having to treat enemy injured as well as our own, the cold, unapologetic hatefulness—especially that of the SS officers—crushed her heart and had her crying herself to sleep every night.

The war ended while she was still abroad and Grandma served for a while in a Paris hospital. Upon returning stateside, Deaconess Hospital—where she went to nursing school—heartily welcomed her back. Her life as a war nurse ended and "life" began anew in Cincinnati.

Some of the surprises I discovered in her diary that she never discussed were, naturally, the horrors she witnessed and had to try and heal. Also, she was eventually promoted to 2nd Lieutenant, and at one point, while with the Red Cross, was managing entire hospital floors. Grandma?

She never wrote or spoke of the tragedy and heartbreak she endured, nor the relationships she had, including an engagement to another soldier who tragically died during the war. It was just another heartbreak compounded by the conflict and strife that surrounded her. To know Grandma was on the cusp of a marriage and possible new life that would not have include me was astounding to discover.

There were plenty of good times, too, and she delights in mentioning those, especially.

Over my lifetime with Grandma, I would get lots of crazy gifts from her, including magnifying glasses ALMOST EVERY YEAR for my birthday. But her diary topped them all.

I hope my family enjoys learning about Grandma's military life in WWII and can see her now as I do: 2nd Lieutenant Arlene Reuter, a brave front line war nurse, veteran, true hero, romantic and young woman about Europe who lived a small lifetime of hardship and worldly experiences.

And I wish that every reader comes to understand a little more about the realities of war and of a beautiful life and the love that weaved through it.

Arlene Reuter (Windhorst)

Ft. Knox, Kentucky

September 1, Tuesday, 1942

1st entry

Ft. Knox 1:15 pm train

Dear diary, We're in the Army now! Arrived safely after a pleasant trip. Waited 2 hours in depot for ambulances. Signed up. Jean and I room together. Met old and new kids, all nice, but sort of on the wild side. Think I'm gonna like it. Hope folks don't worry. We eat in nurse's mess with officers (doctors), Generals & all.

September 2, Wednesday, 1942

Cloudy at times. Had pictures taken for identification & got our 1st tetanus shots. Went to PX in town with Marylou Bass & kids. Was measured for a 45 winter uniform. Went to first military lecture by Col. Von Hook. Visited Stanley in hospital. Went on walk with Marylou Bass' Ward & Ratliff, we talked with some very nice sergeants. Good day.

September 3, Thursday, 1942

Sunny. 1st day on duty. Nice patients. Kidded with us etc. Lt. Pertaly – Ward surgeon – very nice. Had orientation lecture today. Started to go to show tonight. Men everywhere. Oh, to see a woman. Didn't go because we'd seen that. Went to PX and met 2 privates who walked home with us. Think I'm going to like duty.

September 4, Friday, 1942

Misty. Lt. Peabody told me I signed for something we didn't get and he would have to pay for it but he said we could go over to med. supply & explain at supplier. Cute & smart & comes up to talk & stirs my tea & asks about fish. Got 18 year old boy to write to Ruth. Nice & family. Went to lecture by a Major. Got more mail from home.

September 5, Saturday, 1942

Sunny. Cleaned for Saturday inspection Ward. Had to go to medical supply with Lt. Peabody to explain bars & netting. He was very nice. He's from Wisconsin. Got 2 letters from home. Wrote letters & listened to radio. Not many kids out tonight.

September 6, Sunday, 1942

Sunny. Rain in evening. Went to church at Red Cross. New contentment. Good sermon. Was given white treatment. Took pictures on Ward. Izzo ccs Pt. has a date planned for their grad. Dance for me. Tonight Jean & I went on double date with Capt. & Leut. Cute Texan. OCS boy Presbyterian. Didn't smoke. We rode around post.

September 7, Monday, 1942

Sunny. Slept long. Aunt Erna sent me $10. Worked 12:30 – 7:00. We had 8 discharges and 18 patients transferred in. We were busy. They're chasing off some of the Wards & I go to psychiatry. Jean, Mary Lou Bass & I went to see "The Pied Piper" at #1 theater. It was good.

September 8, Tuesday, 1942

Sunny. I am now on 141 psychiatry. Had class periodically all morning. Got gas mask for drill. Went to PX & got commissary card & check cashed & shipped. Worked my hair & Mary Baumgartner called & asked me to go to country club with a Major – edition of New York Times. Steak dinner. Nice time. It rained.

September 9, Wednesday, 1942

Showers. Worked 7-2. Liked it on duty today. Played cards with patients, Leut. & Stanley. Had to take an ambulance for administration to quarters. It was raining so hard. Slept in afternoon. Went to lecture & movies on military courtesies, saluting etc. Stayed in & wrote letters after lecture.

September 10, Thursday, 1942

Sunny. Worked 11-7. Did my washing. We're living on the floor. Like it much better. Went to gas mask drill this afternoon. Got a letter from home & Don got identification card from N.O. Went down to 130 to see old Ward. Only 10 patients left. I think I like 141 better. Listened to radio.

September 11, Friday, 1942

Worked 7-2. We were busy with new patients. Consultations & IG tents, etc. Slept in afternoon. Went to lecture on military law in evening. Then went on triple date with Wilson Taylor. We went to Country Club first then to Murphys. Met the Leut. I was with Sunday evening. He was there also.

September 12, Saturday, 1942

Sunny. Worked 7-2. Went to class at 9. Mom sent coat, spread, etc. Was taking a nap and Major Sweeney called and wanted to know if I wanted to go to the formal & bring a friend for a Canadian friend of his. We had a very nice time. Then went to Country Club & had sandwiches.

September 13, Sunday, 1942

Sunny-hot. Worked 7-12:30 Wright (Cat. Sahig.) talked for 1st time in 2 ½ months (prison patient came back in). I relieved on 129 while they had class. The Major called this afternoon and wanted to go swimming at the country club and then have dinner there. I told him I had plans and stayed home & wrote letters.

September 14, Monday, 1942

Hot-Sunny. Worked 7-9 and 2-7. Rode to surgical Hosp with Kregler for her cold. Went in ambulance then went to PX with Jean & Dot Holstein, we got a ride up with a Captain. Ate lunch up there. Was very busy on Ward with construction. Saw patient get transferred. With them all night. Stayed home & washed. In evening found Stanley & Booth (MP).

14

September 15, Tuesday, 1942

Hot & sunny. Worked 7-2. Played ping pong with patients. Had 1st drill this afternoon back next to medical supply. Capt., 2nd Leut. & Sergeants drilled us. It was fun. Then the medics drilled after us. Went on double date with Jean & Canadian Leut. Ken from Illinois. Doesn't drink or smoke. Very nice. With a car & everything. Drove to E. town, went to show & had lunch. Very nice time.

September 16, Wednesday, 1942

Worked 11-7. Had fun on duty. Booth & Stanley both tried to make dates with me. Went to 1st supper and good looking capt. sat down & talked to me until he could eat. Went to military lecture and then went with Joan & Stanley on triple date. 2 capt's. 1 Leut. Went to friends apartment and drank Cokes. Told jokes. They were really a riot. Very funny.

September 17, Thursday, 1942

Worked 7-2. Poured some all day. Dilz escaped out window during night, therefore Ward in uproar. We're going to have new guards and sergeants. I got 5 letters at noon. 5 discharges including Booth & Stanley. Got GI winter uniform this afternoon & last shots. Jeans family & girlfriend were down and I called home long distance for Margie Orchard.

September 18, Friday, 1942

Showers. Worked 7-12:30. Took Jeans girlfriend Ruth to the bus station and inquired about tomorrow. Went to lecture on military correspondence by Leut. Miller (Algitant). Major Sweeney called and asked me to go to formal tomorrow night. Made date with Jean to go with him to trade plans & get ready for tomorrow.

September 19, Saturday, 1942

Went to bus station at 4:30 am. Rode to Louisville with nice bus driver who offered to buy me a Coke. Got 7:30 bus to Cincinnati. Arrived there at 11:30. Got from city bus & got home at 1:15 pm. Mom, Ruth May and Daddy cried from happiness. Visited neighbors. Had good supper. Went to Grandpa's. Aunt Emma Jean, Uncle Charlie, Kit, Chas, Bonnie, Beth & Dick – everyone was down. Good to be home. Had lunch. Went home to bed.

September 20, Sunday, 1942

Family took me to 5:15 am bus. Arrived in Louisville at 7:30. Got bus for Ft. Knox at 8:00. Bus broke down & changed buses. Arrived in Ft. Knox at 9:15 am. Bag broke. Cake & candy all over floor. Walked to quarters. Worked 12:30-7. Dier was brought in & put in prison. Stanley still AWOL. Stayed in. Washed my hair, etc. We now have guards all over Ward.

September 21, Monday, 1942

Cold again. Slept long. Worked 11-7. Nothing exciting happened. Made copies of wolf poem for guards on Ward. Morris tried to hang himself in latrine at 6 pm. More excitement. I'm scheduled to go on ND Wednesday. 10 nurses left for Camp Campbell. Some others are going to Texas. We all stayed in tonight and messed around.

September 22, Tuesday, 1942

Cool & sunny. Worked 7-2. Enjoyed work on floor today. Morris was acting up again and we had some guard trouble. Drilled this afternoon. Stayed in and washed tonight. Nothing special happened. Red Skelton & Bob Hope on radio.

September 23, Wednesday, 1942

Cool. Worked 7-11. Had fun with patients & Ward surgeons. Had 2nd
tetanus shot. Slept for 2-3 hours. Went to supper and started 1st night
ND 7-7. Major Farmsworth OD & Capt. Schillinger asst. Morris tried
to commit suicide again around 8:00. Good & cute guards on duty put
him in straight jacket, etc. Had good time with Capt. on romp & Capt.
Roberts etc. who came down. I liked the 1st night.

September 24, Thursday, 1942

Cool. Slept till 5. Went to supper then on duty. Jean told me the
Major called & wanted me to go to the HUP. Masteretto was
readmitted at 10 am. The surgeons brought us sandwiches from the
PX. The guard on one romp insists that he will get the night off & take
me to Cincinnati. The docs & nurses had a party & they were telling us
what a good time they had at breakfast. Morris wrote another suicide
note & knocked out one of the guard's teeth out & tried to hang
himself again.

September 25, Friday, 1942

Cool. Got up early & went to see 1550th SU on parade. We took
pictures. It was good. Walked home. Morris banged his head against
the iron door. Snellbacker was telling me about Conley wanting to ask
me for a date but being afraid & that Ratliff is going to ask me too.
Seems odd all of a sudden. But Conley is a darling.

September 26, Saturday, 1942

Rainy. Slept all day. Went on duty at 7:00. Snellbacker's birthday.
Conley and I had to be less friendly than ever because we understood
how we stand & Ratliff put him in front when we're in back and in
back when we're in front. Conley doesn't like it. He waited for me
at the end of the romp at 11:30 & I had already gone at 11:15 pm. I
missed him.

September 27, Sunday, 1942

Cold. Tried to get McIntyre & Payton to go to church with me. They
never did come. It was in the old conliment. Slept late & went on duty.
Quiet night. Conley gave me a clipping from a magazine. "I never
dreamed I'd be the one." He really is cute. I asked for Tuesday off. I
sure hope it turns out ok & that I like him.

September 28, Monday, 1942

Cool. Slept late. I took my radio on duty. Did some work for Capt.
Williams. Typing etc. Snellbacker & Janreshi can't go with us so we
have to go alone. I'm meeting him at 7:30 at the fort. I'm going to wear
blue suit & tan top coat. Snellbacker says he knows he'll go. We have a
new guard on our romp now.

September 29, Tuesday, 1942

Went with kids in ambulance to be reclassified in replacement center.
My day off. Met Conley at 7:30 at corner & we walked to show. Saw
"Somewhere I'll Find You." Clark Gable & Lana Turner. Went to PX
& got soda. Walked home. He walked me right up to the door. Very
nice & affectionate. Held my hand in show.

September 30, Wednesday, 1942

Slept till 2:00. Got up & in uniform. Had to drill. We had fun learning
columns. Left & left, flash etc. Sergeants drilled us. Nothing special.
Worked NP Snellbacker was off & Ratliff shifts were on. I brought
them coffee etc. Had a lot of fun. Conley said he had a great time.

MEMORANDA

Well, no regrets so far. Like it better than at 1st. Met a lot of new people. Haven't been really homesick so far. The Major was very nice to me but Conley is much more my type. Only I'm not taking him seriously. It's kind of fun to go around with him.

October 1, Thursday, 1942

Went to Louisville early with Keagler & other kids. We shopped, had our pictures taken. Ate lunch at the French village. Then went to a bar and had our fortunes told. It was fun. I'm going to have 4 kids. Came home & went right on duty. Very tired. Snellbacker says he thinks Conley wants to marry me. I doubt it.

October 2, Friday, 1942

Warmer. Slept late. Got 4 letters including $1.00 from Mrs. Weiss. Went on duty. Was busy. Had patients have epileptic seizures. Got in new patients. Morris acted up & had other new patients day. 27 altogether. Conley asked me to meet him again at 3:30.

October 3, Saturday, 1942

Slept till 2. Dressed and met Conley down the road. We were going for walk & take pictures but he is restricted to hospital area because of Dunken Barrack orderly. Talked for 1 ½ hours & it started to rain. Went back and ate supper and went on duty. Nothing special happened. Conley tells me he isn't handing me a line but I doubt it.

October 4, Sunday, 1942

Rainy. Went to bed and slept all day. Jean is in Cincinnati for weekend. Murphy (alcoholic) in straight jacket had trouble giving him paraldryl. So far I guess Conley still likes me. Had fun with Ratliff shift on 9. Payton asked me to go to show when I get night off. He is cute also.

October 5, Monday, 1942

Cooler. Slept late. Nothing special happened. Went on duty at 7.
I think Conley still likes me. Tells me he's a one woman man. I doubt
it. Payton came over to see us before he went out on his date. I really
like night duty a lot. We have a lot of fun. Got Slater and guard to
write to Jean & Snellbacker to write to Aunt Etta.

October 6, Tuesday, 1942

Cool. Slept all day. Snellbacker's night off. Benard asked me to go out
with a friend of hers Thursday. But I won't be off. Conley wanted me
to go out with him tomorrow. Tonight's his night off but I have to drill
4-5. I don't know if I like him or not. I got my stuff from util. mills. We
got another S/Sgt. @ 2:30 am. Wild 6 fellows brought him in.

October 7, Wednesday, 1942

Warmer. Slept long. Had trouble with Mexican trying to get out
& striking guards. Ratliff shift. Payton asked me to go out again.
Snellbaker said Slater wants him to fix up a date with him for me.
Sgt. Herman said Conley was waiting for me this morning at 7:00 am
at the end of the romp. None of the patients slept well. We had to put
Mexican in restraint sheet.

October 8, Thursday, 1942

Warmer. Stayed up and went up with Jean to PX. Shopped & ate
lunch in PX. Went to bed & slept late. Got 4 letters from Conley &
Aunt Erna. Quiet night. Snellbaker said Conley said that he would do
anything in the world for me. 31 patients now. 6 new ones. I signed all
night long with Payton & McIntyre.

October 9, Friday, 1942

Cool. Got things ready for tomorrow. Conley gave me the sweetest 3 page letter. Walked over to hall with me. We were busy with Terry chanting religiously all night. Had fun with Slater, trying to throw water on each other. Rushed off duty at 6:00 am.

October 10, Saturday, 1942

Cool. Left on 8:15 bus for Cincinnati. Went with Kaegler. 1st time in uniform. Went up to Good Sam, saw all the kids, Betty, Larry etc. Daddy picked me up. After supper went to Aunt Erna's & grandparents & then to Aunt Freda's. Dickie had surprise party. Everyone liked my uniform.

October 11, Sunday, 1942

Pretty. Went to church and saw everyone. Have 1st Leut. and Corp was there too. Hurried home. Left early for bus station. Picked up Aunt Erna & Jean & then met Betty at bus station. Ruth May came back with us. Then went to show with Jean. I went on duty at 7pm.

October 12, Monday, 1942

Cool. Came off duty & walked Ruth May & them up to PX, country club etc. Got my snapshots & shopped. I ate lunch then walked back & called cab for them to leave at 2 pm. Then I went to sleep. Conley walked me to Mess at 11pm & had fun with Payton & McIntyre on Ratliff shift.

October 13, Tuesday, 1942

Cool. Slept all day. 9 hours. Quiet night. Conley gave me another letter. I have decided if I go with him tomorrow night it will be the last time and better for the both of us. I'm beginning to get jittery and to feel a little tied down.

October 14, Wednesday, 1942

Cool. Worked in am. Slept late. Got new GI sweater. Paid for Coke I owed Campbell on hel. Had trouble with Terry, he thinks he's Jesus, Ian, Mary & Slater is. Conley walked me to night supper & asked me for a date tomorrow night. I told him it would probably be the last one & he went up in the air & asked why I didn't tell him in the beginning etc. I felt bad.

October 15, Thursday, 1942

Had fun during night with Slater. Terry kept calling him Jacob & wouldn't let either one of us leave him. Went to bed. Slept till 3pm. Went over & got last tetanus shots. We got our dog tags today. Ate supper with Jean and met Conley at 7pm. We went to theater #3 again. Dumb show. "Sin Town" Connie Bennett. Walked home. He kissed me. We have an understanding. He really is swell.

October 16, Friday, 1942

Pretty. Slept till noon. Dressed and went to PX. with Jean. Came home & ate supper. Worked 7-7. Nothing exciting happened. Lembegeder said he knew all about Conley & myself & some more. Payton asked me to go to the show with him again. He said if I moved off the floor he'd go "over the hill". Conley told me last night if I didn't go with him anymore he'd sign for foreign service.

October 17, Saturday, 1942

Pretty. Washed my hair. Worked 7-7. Nothing special happened. Terry & Renteria, neither one slept all night. Paul Cook (guard) was put in guard house for burning matters & Sgt. Herman was taken off. We had 2 new men on. Nothing exciting happened.

October 18, Sunday, 1942

Beautiful day. Met Betty Marten & her girlfriends at the bus station & showed them everything. Ate at the PX, showed them the Ward etc. Durham and Snellbaker were going to take them to the show if they could stay but they left at 7:00. Had fun on duty with Conley & Sgt. McIntyre on AD then with Slater & new Sgt. Kattus on ND. They are swell.

October 19, Monday, 1942

Last night on night duty. Payton got a letter from Ruth May. He asked me about 10 times when I was going to the show with him. He has a cold. Had very quick night. Had a lot of fun with Slater & Sgt. Kotus. Slater played with my hair all night.

October 20, Tuesday, 1942

Dressed & went to PX & central mess with Kaegler. We played the slot machines. Met Slater walking up to PX and then again when we went to hospital PX. He really is cute. Was going on date with Julian but French went anyhow. Stayed home & washed & took OD for Wilson. Nothing special happened.

October 21, Wednesday, 1942

Day duty. When I walked on the floor the group all started "You Are My Sunshine" Worked 7-9 & 2-7. It was sort of fun being on day duty again. Didn't work hard except helped on 136 open new Ward from 6-7. Went for walk with Kaegler to PX. Met Slater as he was coming back, he didn't notice us. Parontanell called me twice to come to Red Cross Recreation Hall for dance.

October 22, Thursday, 1942

Had a PM. Was on by myself this morning. Was going to Louisville & Payton was supposed to go too but it rained all afternoon & I called his barracks & we didn't go. Stayed in and read then went over to the recreation hall about 8:30. They had had a tea for Dore (Capt) who is leaving. We danced and sang.

October 23, Friday, 1942

Ate lunch & then went on duty. Capt. Williams had birthday cake.
Codie leaving for Atesburg. Snellbaker & other bunch are going, we
were all saying good bye. Payton said he was really going yesterday &
that he was disappointed. Conley came back & made a date for show
#3. It was fairly good. We walked. I have a cold. He is very amorous &
affectionate.

October 24, Saturday, 1942

Had a day off. Was supposed to double date (Formal) but Benjy talked
me into going with a friend of the Major & I got a date with Kaegler
for the other fellow. They had taxi trouble so we walked over. 1st Leut.
Don Thomas, wonderful, swell dancer from Oregon. Leut. Lewis. Tall,
reminded me of Farrels type.

October 25, Sunday, 1942

Slept late. Didn't go to church cause I didn't have any stockings to
wear. Went on at 12:30-7. Worked 138 to relieve for Kilso's day off.
Wrote letters. Stopped down on 141. Then picked Julian up on 131 &
discovered Sgt. Herman, a patient Ester saw last night as we walked past
show. Darn it he didn't call.

October 26, Monday, 1942

Worked 7-9 & 2-7. It was very cold. Worked in AM. In afternoon we
were acting silly & they left me Morris on strap by myself & he tried to
get away & hit Conley on the jaw, later on Renteria scratched him &
Homblin hit him in the chest. Stayed home in evening after meeting &
read. Gave officers a note for Conley.

October 27, Tuesday, 1942

Worked 7-12:30 then got my clothes ready. Conley called & I met him at
the bus station. We went to Louisville on 4 pm bus. It was held up until
5:30. Took Jean's picture back to Stewarts & then went to show & saw
Charlie McCarthy. Ate in bus station & got 9:30 bus back. In at 11:15 pm.

October 28, Wednesday, 1942

2-7 off drilled. Nothing special happened. Lt. Thomas called Cates & asked for a date & when she couldn't go he asked for any 3 to go. French went with him. Kaegler & I went for a walk & stopped in central mess. Was I down on men. Then we stopped & talked to Cpl. Rahts & guard out front. Conley called and wanted to go out. They took a guard off each shift, good ones. McIntyre, Slater & Conley. Ratliff knew all about Conley and myself.

October 29, Thursday, 1942

Worked 11-7. Had fun on duty with Sgt. Koch & Eisler & kids. Had a date with Conley at 8 & when I walked down the street Sgt. Turners sister in-law stopped in cat & hollered & asked him to go for a ride. At the same time a Lt. met me & asked me to go to the country club. Conley then walked me down to meet him. They saluted each other. It was funny. He's trying for Capt. now. Tried to break off with Conley again but he was sweeter than ever. I think I really like him now.

October 30, Friday, 1942

Had a 2-7 off. It rained all day. Usual good time on duty. I like it now. Was going to stay home & was to fix Dot's hair but Eva Julian called & wanted me to go with her on double date with 2 2nd Lt's. One was Lt. Miller & the other Lt. Morris. I was with Morris. We went to Murphy's. Had a good time, but not wonderful.

October 31, Saturday, 1942

Cool. Halloween. Worked 11-7. Nothing special happened on duty. Went to Louisville with Betty Kaegler & Paul Bruster on a double date. They have a swell car & we had oodles of fun. Laughed until I cried. Went to Orchestra & guest singer in armed forces from Tommy Dorsey's orchestra. We rode around and got in around 1:15 am.

MEMORANDA

I like the army better all the time except we don't get to go with whomever we want and I can't seem to break off with Conley. There are more cadre's leaving and about 18 sgts. Going to Texas this week.

November 1, Sunday, 1942

Pretty. Had a 7-12:30. Had fun arguing with Sgts. Koch & Kruger.
Julian & I went to Louisville in uniform & did we have to salute. Ate in
French village. Couldn't get into show so went to Walgreens, then went
to see J. McDonald. Had fun coming home on bus & then got a ride
from bus station with 3 1550th fellows.

November 2, Monday, 1942

Rain. Slept late. Worked 11-7. Had fun fighting with Sgt. Koch. His
last day before a furlough. Called long distance on duty & nobody was
home but Ruth May. We talked for a long while. Bernard asked me to go
on double date with her Wednesday. Had a date with Conley. Went to
show. Double feature. He is swell.

November 3, Tuesday, 1942

Had a 9-2 off. Koch, Patten & Riddick were all dismissed. Payton
wanted me to go to Louisville with him again. Nothing special happened
on or off duty. Payton came over about 7pm & walked down romp with
me. Stayed in & washed hair & darned socks etc. Listened to radio.

November 4, Wednesday, 1942

Had a 7-2. Was supposed to drill but didn't. Payton is still asking for a
date. He gets mad when I tell him I can't go. Went on double date with
B. Bernard & Alabaster. I was with a 1st Lt., Charlie Kell. Very nice.
Good dancer – not even affectionate. We went to country club then
danced at brick club then Murphy's. Charlie had to bring us home.
Alabaster & Bernard got into a fight.

November 5, Thursday, 1942

Rained. Had a 12:30 off. Went to Louisville with Jean, Julian & Kaegler.
We shopped. I got a red dress. Then I met Conley at bus station at 6 pm
and we went to see the "Major & the Minor" then went to Thompson's.
We had to wait on bus and we had a wonderful ride home. We didn't get
home till 12:30 am & had trouble getting taxi in rain. Jean had to wait &
come get us.

November 6, Friday, 1942

Rain for a change. Had an 11-7. Longley was discharged & a 1st Lt. & 1 Sgt. Came after him and Surkin insulted him at the same time I received my mom's telegram over the phone. I had to relieve or help on 136 from 5-7. Then Julian begged me to go with her so she could be 1st Lt. Condiff. I went with Sgt. Johnston, who was nice. We had fun arguing.

November 7, Saturday, 1943

Rained. Worked 7-2. Met mom at bus station at 7pm. She was an hour late. It was raining & messy & the place was packed. I took her to the PX to eat & then to theater #1. We left the suitcase in the front office. We had to wait in lobby over an hour. There were 3 cute Lt.'s waiting too. A Texan walked us home and carried our suitcase.

November 8, Sunday, 1942

Cloudy. Worked 7-12:30. Took mom to church at 9:15 then on the Ward. We went to dinner at the country club with Jean's sister & friends & met same 3 Lt.'s. Then Jean, Mary, mom & I went riding around, came home & ate in our mess hall after going back up on the Ward. In the evening met Conley & he took us to the show. Walked & then went down 141 to see Jean again.

November 9, Monday, 1942

Beautiful day. Had a 9-2 off. Went on at 6:00 for Jean & they drove mom home. Then I went over & ate breakfast about 7:30. Slept from 10-1. Sgt. Johnson, the one I was with the other night called on duty. I relieved on 138 for drill. Bernard said Capt. Goodman wants a date with me. Got a letter from Sgt. Koch from Nebraska. Cute kid. Went to show with Conley. It was windy.

November 10, Tuesday, 1942

Cold & very windy & rainy this am. Worked 7-12:30. Turned out pretty in afternoon but very cold. 22 more kids are leaving. Don't know where?? Went to Louisville with Julian. Shopped & then ate in Kunz's. Then went to see "Springtime in the Rockies." Very good.

November 11, Wednesday, 1942

Had a 7-2. Nothing special happened. Got a letter from home &
Betty Mates & a card from Don. Drilled 4-5. Sgt. Hall drilled us.
Messed around until 8:00 pm. Met Conley & we went to see "Tales of
Manhattan." Wonderful. I still like him a lot. He just does something to
me. Wish he would get another rating.

November 12, Thursday, 1942

Slept long. Had an 11-7. Sgt. Johnson called again & wanted me to go to
a big farewell shindig they're giving some fellows. Floor show, good food
etc. but I told him I couldn't go. He called on duty. Stayed in and washed
my hair. 22 nurses are leaving Saturday. Port of embarkation NY city
destination unknown.

November 13, Friday, 1942

Betty Kaegler's birthday. Had a 9-2 off. Worked on 309, moved it to
H-49. Good Ward. It was good experience. Then went back on 141
& had fun with Ersler & Alford. Met Conley at 8 & went to see Betty
Davis in "Now, Voyager." It was wonderful. And I did cry. Conley is a
swell kid.

November 14, Saturday, 1942

Had a 7-2. Went to PX with Jean, Kaegler & Julian in uniform. Ate at
bus station & then went to see the 22 kids off at the train station. There
was a crowd there & it was very touching. Went back and played slot
machines at Central Mess. Stayed home in evening. Dave (Dot's friend)
was home on weekend.

November 15, Sunday, 1942

Had a 7-2 & asked Durham to tell Conley to meet me at 7 instead of 8
& he didn't get to see him so I was early & I went down on 141 & talked
with Jean. Payton's shift was on. Then Conley came in & we talked then
went to the show & saw "Seven Sweethearts." Then went back on the
Ward & walked Jean to night supper. Sgt. Gulman & whole shebang.

November 16, Monday, 1942

Warmer. Worked 11-7. Campbell came over to visit us on the floor, he is out of the hospital. I told Jean that I wasn't going to meet Conley tonight. It was too often, etc. & he came up on the Ward & she told him everything I said. We tried to call him & couldn't find him & he came back up on Ward & we made a date for tomorrow night. Got a letter from home.

November 17, Tuesday, 1942

Worked 7-2 on H-138. Helped Capt. Stevens with 2 spinals. In afternoon woman gave Deb & I locha facial & sold us creams. Wore my red dress & triple dated with Cpl. Roberts, Cpl. Paul, Kerlein & Julian & Conley & myself. We went to #1 theater & saw stage show. Then watched basketball game & went to bowling alley. We had more fun.

November 18, Wednesday, 1942

Had a 9-2 off. Saw Sgt. Koch for 1st time since he's back from furlough. Was busy. Admitted 1 patient, transferred in 3. Messed around in evening & then walked up PX with Jean, Halstein & Beitz. We had fun. Before that I walked over with Robertson & Paul to meet the gals.

November 19, Thursday, 1942

Had a PM. Went to Louisville with Jean, Betty & Ema. Did a little shopping. As soon as we came out of the bus station we met Conley but then I met him again at 6. We went to the French village & met Jean. Had a turkey supper. Then we went to double feature. They picked us up in a great big car & we rode 9 miles to "The Colonel." They had a floor show. Conley & I had a wonderful time. I don't know if Jean did or not. We didn't get in until 2 am. I couldn't help it I let him kiss me 5 times. I was sleepy.

November 20, Friday, 1942

Rainy all day. Worked 7-3 & really worked. Had a patient have 3 seizures & was busy all around. The kids in the 91st are pulling out. We had an official bulletin that we do not wear civilian clothes, not even formals. The bottom fell out of my world. I guess that finished Conley & I. I cried for 3 solid hours. I guess maybe I was really in love for the first time. Wrote a letter to him to give to him from Sgt. Harmann & wrote a letter home. Stayed home & was miserable.

November 21, Saturday, 1942

Rained all day. Worked 7-11 & 3-7. Did some real nursing again for a change. Sick patients & was busy. Went with Kaegler on blind date. Didn't want to. Didn't have a very good time. Played ping pong in the day room. Had to go in uniform.

November 22, Sunday, 1942

Worked 7-12. Rained again. Saw Conley in the hall. Don't think I'll ever get over him. He was really sweet & I'll know I'll never get to go with him again. Slept this afternoon. Then washed & then went to PX & saw show. "Nightime" #4 (one sacred spot) with Jean, Kaegler & Julian. We had fun. Laughed until we almost cried.

November 23, Monday, 1942

Rain again & colder. Worked 7-2. Capt. Stevens wants me to stay there instead of going to 128. Got a letter from Betty & another poem & a letter from Jean B. We went up PX & bought fast lockers & I bought candy & sent it home. Got candy from Aunt Etta. Stayed home and wrote letters etc. with kids. Didn't see or hear from Conley.

November 24, Tuesday, 1942

Rainy & cold. Worked 7-8 & 12:30-7. We weren't busy. Conley called me on duty & wanted me to go out anyway. I met him on the romp this morning too. I got his letter at noon. Sgt. Koch also called & talked for about an hour & then I met him in the PX when I went with Jean & then he came down on the Ward for about 1 ½ hrs. Insisting that I go out with him. Stayed home & wrote letters.

November 25, Wednesday, 1942

Beautiful day. We all had PM's. Conley is leaving on a Cadre. I never had so many lumps in my throat. He called & we made a date for tonight. Jean, Dot, Eve & I went to PX for a supper after bowling. We went to show and saw Abbott & Costello. Tried to say good bye & I cried so we made it again for tomorrow. 17th date with him. I really think I'm in love with him.

November 26, Thursday, 1942

Cold. Thanksgiving. Was called to nursing office to leave on foreign duty at anytime. Had physical & talked to Capt. Pohle etc. The 91st is pulling out also. Koch called up to say good bye. Conley came up on duty with another letter & then went down to see Jean for a while. Met him at 8 & we went to show "7 Days Gone." It was very cold. Most wonderful time I've had. We said good bye. I cried & cried. Couldn't help it. So confused and mixed up. He told me he loves me and wants to marry me when it's over.

November 27, Friday, 1942

Cold. Today was the day. Had a 9-2 off & had my lab work done. Went to PX with Jean & got some of my things ready. Glimpsed at Conley in the hall, he was laughing. His cadre & the 91st unit left at 4:50 pm on the train. Felt blue. Worked till 7. Did some packing in the evening. Called long distance from the Ward.

November 28, Saturday, 1942

Cold. Worked 7-9 on 138 & then 9-2 on H-52. We were very busy. Went to signal office & got my money. Had my allotment made out & drew up a will. Came back and had Christmas presents from home & Aunt Erna. Practical things. Received a letter from Conley already from Louisville. Ema wanted me to go on a double date with her. They were cute but ignorant dates & we walked out on them.

November 29, Sunday, 1942

Cold. Slept late. Worked 12:30-7. Had a nice time on duty. Nice patients. One patient gave me $1.00 as a going away present. Sgt. Hall asked me for a date & a lot of the other kids wanted me to go on a blind date with them but I had too much to do.

November 30, Monday, 1942

Had a PM. Worked till 12:30. Got letters from home. Went to Knox beauty parlor & got a permanent then went to bank & cashed check. Came home in cab with other kid. Went back up to PX with Jean, Ema & her friend. Got a ride up with a Lt. Bought family presents at the PX & ate at the bus station.

MEMORANDA

A wonderful but sad month. Really learned to like Conley a lot & hated to see him go but it probably was for better. It may be love or close to it. Hope I see him again but I doubt if I ever will. He is a wonderful, sweet boy.

Like the army very much now. Don't think I'd like civilian life at all until the war's over except to be with the family. I'm beginning to understand me now and have met some swell people but the army kind of tears your emotions apart shipping people off all the time. I sure miss Conley.

December 1, Tuesday, 1942

Very cold. Had a 9-2 off. Was pretty busy in afternoon. 2 spinals. Major Gustafson was really kept busy. Jean & Ema had PM's & went to Louisville. Stayed home & washed & listened to radio. Didn't get a letter from Conley & feel blue since Jean told me about the way Dot's Ray was acting all ready.

December 2, Wednesday, 1942

Snow & very cold & windy. 7-8 & 12:30-7. Have nice cute patients. They gave Miss Hall nurse a dresser set for her birthday. Got a very sweet letter from Conley. He is on Staten Island N.Y. & still loves and misses me. Stayed in and wrote him a letter & messed around with Jean & Casey. Have no desire to go out. The boys we were with Saturday have been restricted.

December 3, Thursday, 1942

Had a 7-2. Bunch of patients. Full house. Slept in afternoon. Met Ema & Jean at PX & ate supper there & then ate in our dining room. Bought Daddy an Esquire. Went down Red Cross & had them play the wave song one of our patients wrote. Met Payton for a minute or two in hall. Stayed home in evening with Ema & Jean.

December 4, Friday, 1942

Had a 9-2 off. Slept & mailed things home. Was busy on duty. Very busy. I like Major Gustafson a lot. He's a brilliant man. Ema & Jean each received a letter from Conley & he sounds as though he doesn't like it & that he still loves me. He asked all about me. Stayed home & wrote home.

December 5, Saturday, 1942

Snow & rain. Had a 7-2 & had inspection on Ward this am. Got another letter from Conley this noon & he still hadn't heard from me. Sgt. Koch pulled up & wanted me to go out again. Called in our quarters. He's cute, we talked for a while. I wouldn't go. Went over & ate supper. Got a box of cookies from the church. Stayed in and washed my hair & wrote a letter to Conley with jokes & poems.

December 6, Sunday, 1942

Slept too late to go to church. Worked 12:30-7. Koch & Ensler were
acting silly, calling up & came down & took some pictures of me on duty.
We had more fun on duty. Koehler (PT) played his piano acordian &
we had a regular party. I danced with Hoad (cute patient from Bowman
Field). Ema, Jean & I triple dated later & had a fair time.

December 7, Monday, 1942

Snow again. We're working 8 hours now. Patients were all cute, teasing
me about last night. Got another letter from Conley. (sweet) Also
got a card from Maher, one of my old patients from '38. Cute from
Washington. Had to go see 1st military movie at #1. Then went to PX &
met Jean. We shopped. Ema & kids from 15th are on the alert. Wrote to
Conley.

December 8, Tuesday, 1942

The 15th is leaving tomorrow. We are now working one girl on a floor
12 hours. Nice cute patients on 138 but I was tired. Received 1 dozen
bars of good soap from alumnae with Coke & stationary from home.
Came over & helped kids pack etc. Said goodbyes etc. Nothing unusual
happened.

December 9, Wednesday, 1942

Worked 7-3. Kids all running around ready to leave. Got a lot of
mail today. Went to train depot & saw Ema & all 42 kids of 15th
off. It was gloomy. Went to PX afterWards and Sgt. Engle O.P. of
Major Gustafson's brought us home. He is very nice. Looks like Fred
McMurray. Tired, went to bed early.

December 10, Thursday, 1942

Had an 11-3 off. Worked with Potner. She & Gus are both swell. Have
a small bunch of patients. Got another letter from Conley and a special
delivery from home saying that they would be down soon. Stayed home
& wrote letters & washed.

December 11, Friday, 1942

Worked 7-3. Discharged 6 of our best patients. Took all the others to see "Prelude to War" in Red Cross building. Sat with Hoad & Huglun. Had fun. Got $5 from camp Ward church, a letter from Betty from home & 2 from Conley. Stayed in & wrote to him & washed etc. The whole quarter stayed in & listened to radio.

December 12, Saturday, 1942

Worked 7-11 & 3-7. Major Nimity was inspector. Had fun on Ward. Have temp of 99.6 & sore throat & feel achy all over. Got a letter from Aunt Etta. It's very cold & nasty. Was going with Jean but decided I was too tired. Called long distance about tomorrow. Hope they can come.

December 13, Sunday, 1942

Worked 7-12:30. Met family at 2 pm. Took them to bus station then walked them around & back to quarters. Took them over to the Ward & they met Portner. Then took them to PX & back to bus. They didn't stay long. Went to country club with Lt. Bonesteal & Shantley & Lt. Larson. Shantley & Larson fought the whole time.

December 14, Monday, 1942

Had a 9-12:30 off & Portner had a PM. Had fun with Hoad, Burns, Jenkins etc. Got an air mail letter from Conley. Jean went to Louisville. Got a beautiful Christmas card from Conley. Stayed home & wrote letters & fixed my feet. Nothing unusual happened.

December 15, Tuesday, 1942

Worked 7-3. Discharged Hoad & 2 others. Had fun on the Ward as usual. Like to work with Portner. Washed in afternoon. Went to theater #1 & saw Blackstone the magician with Kaegler & Portner. Went to PX coffee shop & got a ride home in jeep.

December 16, Wednesday, 1942

Had a 11-3 off. Got a letter from Conley. Nothing very, very unusual happened. Had fun on duty as usual. Got a ride up to bus station with MP & met Alma & took her to PX then got a cab home & we all talked & then took Alma over to a room in 7 in which to sleep. I wrote a letter to Conley.

December 17, Thursday, 1942

Had a 9-3 off. Stopped in PX with Jean on way off duty & talked to a bunch of the fellows then took Alma to bus station cafeteria with Kaegler & then to PX & put her on 2:15 bus. Came back & went on duty & worked till 8:30 pm. Ensler put his picture up. Stayed in again.

December 18, Friday, 1942

Worked 7-12:30. Came off duty & visited Janosky with Jean. Jean had a PM also. Slept in afternoon. Stayed in & wrote letters & thank you's. Got a lot more cards but didn't hear from Conley for 2 days which makes me very unhappy.

December 19, Saturday, 1942

Worked 7-9 & 12:30-7. Had fun with Lt. pt. & other pts. It was miserable out, cold & sleety. Walked to PX with Kaegler & Portner & then went to show and saw double feature & horrible mummy pretune. Had to walk home too.

December 20, Sunday, 1942

Worked 7-3. Gus is swell to work with. Got letters from Ema & Conley among Christmas cards. Got a box of candy & a pillow cover from Conley. Stayed home with cold & washed my hair & messed around. The kids were all in & came down to my room.

December 21, Monday, 1942

Worked 7-3. Was busy all day. Transfers out & admissions etc. Got a lot more cards. Have a very bad cold. Stayed in all afternoon & slept. Wrote cards in evening. Jean & Portner went to movie & brought me sandwich.

December 22, Tuesday, 1942

Rainy. Worked 7-9:30 & 3-8:30. Received 2 letters from Conley among others in noon mail & dresser set from him special delivery in evening. Had a fun duty as usual. Major Gustafson is leaving today on a 3 day pass. Worked till 9 & then wrote letters etc. Nothing unusual happened.

December 23, Wednesday, 1942

Rainy. Worked 7-9 & 12:30-7. Had fun with the Lt. & I met boys in the PX. Jean & I walked up to the PX & sent poinsettia plants home & then ate & then took a cab with a Lt. in it who wanted to take us to Murphy's.

December 24, Thursday, 1942

Worked 7-3. Got a compost from Bruno, Yordleys from Steinworth & soup from Bozzell. Opened presents in afternoon. We were having an egg nog party & 3 Lts. walked in & 6 of us went with them to the Brick club. Had a swell time & then went to church with Francis & then walked around & home. They are swell kids & said they'd call me. Had a good Christmas Eve.

Arlene on far left.

December 25, Friday, 1942

Worked split until 11am on 128 with Kaegler, Bill, Conley's friend. Then had a delicious dinner. They told me I was going on ND on 141. Slept & then went back to 138 from 3-7. Had fun with the patients as usual. Went to show with Kaegler & Portner at #1.

December 26, Saturday, 1942

Worked 7-12:30 on 138. Had inspection. Said goodbye to all the patients that came over. Slept some. Then went on ND. 141 again. Payton, Zimba were on again. Then Sgt. Sullivan worked night as relief. We had fun doing card tricks etc. Got another letter from Conley.

December 27, Sunday, 1942

Slept until 5. Then got ready & went to mess. Got another letter from Conley. Went on duty at 7 & Kilhourne went up on guards. Sgt. Zimba has his hand and wrist in cast. They had to send new guards. Gulman came over & stayed a while & called up & we had a lot of fun. Received a small Christmas box from Aunt Erna.

December 28, Monday, 1942

Rain again. Slept all day. Another letter from Conley. Had fun 7-7 as usual. Gulman & Sgt. Green were both over for a long while & called up & I wrote letters etc. Nothing unusual.

December 29, Tuesday, 1942

Rain again. Slept late. Another letter from Conley. Had fun as usual. Gulman & Green both called up. I just about have Gulman fixed up with Kennedy, my relief. Gulman wants me to double date with Green.

December 30, Wednesday, 1942

Slept all day as per usual. Another letter from Conley. Had fun with kids on duty & kids off duty. Nothing unusual.

December 31, Thursday, 1942

Fine New Years Eve on ND & we did have fun. Ride calling up etc. Lt. Lind called 3 times from AFRT and wants me to go out. Gulman was up for a while & everyone was around.

MEMORANDUM

Eventful year. Started working ND in nursery at Good Sam, down to psych, where we had oodles of fun to joining the Army. Meeting Conley among many other swell people. Here's hoping this hateful war is over next year at this time.

January 1, Friday, 1943

Slept all day. Received 2 letters from Conley. Went on duty & had visitors & phone ringing continuously. Brickfield, Zimmerman OCS, Nichols, Nightingale all from 138 were up. Maj. Shiler was OD. The Lt. called 3 times & wants me to go to dinner Sun.

January 2, Saturday, 1943

Didn't sleep well. Too much noise. Lt. Lind called about 4pm & wanted me to go out with him. Then he called on duty twice & was coming over. I wouldn't go with him because I washed my hair & was too tired. Got 2 letters from Conley. He still is the sweetest ever.

January 3, Sunday, 1943

Slept late. The boys came up & visited etc. Got a letter from Conley & one from home telling me Grandpa Reuter is so sick. Nothing unusual happened. Had fun with Sgts.

January 4, Monday, 1943

Slept late. Went on at 7. Wrote letters etc. Major Sailer & Lt. Scholl came up & were acting silly, wanted room etc. Sgt. Green called up & talked for 1 hour from 9-10. Nothing unusual happened. Had fun with Sgt. Delucia again.

January 5, Tuesday, 1943

Beautiful day. Got up & cleaned my room a little. Went to mess then on duty. Alford is back on 3-11 shift & Payton went on days & came over to visit last night. Got 6 letters, 2 from Conley & one of them from Uncle Bill. Lt. Lind called & is leaving for Ft. Benning.

January 6, Wednesday, 1943

Slept late. Did the usual thing on night duty. Kids called up. 139 visited. Had fun with Deluera & kids. Read Deterra's book he gave me.

January 7, Thursday, 1943

Slept late. Got a letter from Conley, mad at me for believing lies the fellows told me & then got 2 other letters from him apologizing. We had a blackout & the patients from 139 came up. Had fun. Stopped on 139 in morning. 3-11 shifts if fun. Sgt. Miller & Alfords.

January 8, Friday, 1943

Overslept and didn't go to mess. Patients from 139 visited. I had fun playing cards with Sgt. Miller & kids, Alfords, Agie. Swell bunch of kids. Sgt. Gulman called up & then had fun when Gulman came over. Sgt. Carter came up to visit me.

January 9, Saturday, 1943

Had to get up early & go to detach & supply for the rest of my uniforms & met Sgt. Hall & Bonestreet then walked to romp with Capt. Williams & Major Gustafson & hollered at us & teased about the bet. Then I met Deluera & Deterra & had to go back to the PX & then met Sgt. Miller, Alford & Agie & treated them all to cake. Got a letter from Conley.

January 10, Sunday, 1943

Went to church with Rynee in old cont. It was nice. Came back and washed. Sgt. Miller worked 16 hour night. Sgt. Carter called again & DeLucia & Sgt. Gulman called 3 times from NCO club with Kennedy & Rymer. They came up & we met them on the romp & we were going to night supper. Had fun with Miller.

January 11, Monday, 1943

Overslept. Didn't get up till 6. Got 2 letters from Conley. Had fun on duty as usual. Zimmerman, Cantrell & Deterra were up as usual. Deterra brought up pictures for me. Was talking to him, he got a letter from Mehr & he said he was mad at me. He gave me one of Mehr's pictures. He is a cute kid.

January 12, Tuesday, 1943

My last night on night duty. Had fun as usual. Sgt. Gulman came up & gave me his pictures etc.

January 13, Wednesday, 1943

Started on 9:30 on Knox bus & then 11am bus to Cincy. Rode all the way with a fellow who was getting a CDD. He was from Harmond. Then family met me at the station & we went to Aunt Erna's, then home & with neighbors then see grandparents. Grandpa Reuter very sick. Left Cincy on 9pm bus & arrived Ft. Knox at 11pm.

January 14, Thursday, 1943

Started new floor. H-131. General Melicino. Nice patients. Worked 7-9 L30 & 3-7 there. Delura & Gulman & Captain "Biel" came in to see me. Then went to work 7-8:30 on H-141. Had fun with Alfords & Nichols, Zimmerman & Contrall & Deterra came down to see me. Then I went down to meet Kaegler & them. I was very tired.

January 15, Friday, 1943

Had a PM. Enjoyed Ward today. Took down isolation sheets etc. Wrote letters, read etc. Went to mess. with Jean and Portner & Major Gustafson teased me about the 80th again. Then we went to #1 theater & saw Joan Crawford in "Reunion in France." It was wonderful. Then we went to PX.

January 16, Saturday, 1943

Got another letter from Conley. Worked 7-11 & 3-7. DeLucia was up on the Ward half dozen times. Had to go to nursing office with Jean about us complaining about our rooms. Stayed home & read & wrote letters etc. Jean had 2 girlfriends down from Cincy.

January 17, Sunday, 1943

Worked 7-3 on the Ward. Had fun. Jean's friends left & we stayed in & read etc. & wrote letters. Nothing unusual.

January 18, Monday, 1943

Had a 7-3. I'm beginning to like 131. We have a new Ward man. Went to PX with Portner & then back to mess. Went to symphony with kids. Cincinnati Eugene Georens & Field House went & came in cab. Packed. Then went to bus station with kids & had hamburgers.

January 19, Tuesday, 1943

Worked 7-8 on 131 & 8-9:30am on H2. Gave a dentist a bath etc. Then had a 9:30-4 off & worked again on H2 until 6 & then relieved on 111. Nurses Ward. Then went back to H2 until 8:30 because of lectures. We were very busy on all of the Wards. DeLucia was over & Gulman called me 3 times.

January 20, Wednesday, 1943

Had a PM – 7-12:30. Ate lunch then went to Louisville with Portner, Rymer & B. Borag & Westfell. Met Hoad at bus station. He is going to Fla. & OCS. Met Leppart in town. She is at Bowman Field. Bought shoes & ate at Canary Cottage, then to show.

January 21, Thursday, 1943

Had an 8:30 to 2:30 off. Had to go to war show at #1 then we ate at bus station grill. Worked till 7 on 131 then on 136-38 & 40. Was busy all over. Then visited on 141 and Sgt. Miller just about mauled me to death. Then went down on 139 & they had a party. Zimmerman & McCormick & then went off with Kaegler.

January 22, Friday, 1943

Had an 11-3 off. Was busy. Got a lot done in evening. Washed hair, clothes, cleaned shoes etc. A lot of kids stayed in & we messed around in quarters.

January 23, Saturday, 1943

Worked 7-3. Had usual good time on duty. Went with Knauer & 2 friends of hers to E-town country club & had a delicious chicken supper & danced & had a community sing. Nice time. We got home at about 2am. Biggerstaff was sick when we came in.

January 24, Sunday, 1943

Had a 9-12:30 off. Went to church with 15 of our patients. Got my navy blue dress through mail. Had fun on duty. 1st Sgts. Stripes from one of my patients around & on 141 & showed them I demanded respect etc. Wrote letters in evening.

January 25, Monday, 1943

Worked 7-10:30 & 2:30-7. We were busy. But had fun on duty. Got off at 7 & went to bus station with Portner & Jean. Came home and danced & exercised in our living room with a bunch of our kids. Then it started to snow at 11pm so we changed from PJ's to shirts & sweaters & went out in snow. Had snow ball fight & had our faces mashed. It was fun. Beautiful.

January 26, Tuesday, 1943

Worked 7-9:30 & went to PX & met Sgt. Gulman & Deterra & patients etc. Bought Deterra a malted milk & 2 sandwiches & then went to bed for a while. Had fun on duty. Miss Brom & I both worked till 7. Sgt. DeLucia, Payton, Zimmerman & Carter & all were down to visit me. Worked 7-8:30 on 23 & 34 & Ray Slater was a hard patient of mine. We had a regular reunion.

January 27, Wednesday, 1943

Had a PM. Lots of fun on duty. Swell patients. Come off wrote Conley. Read & slept & washed. Wore my new dress (navy blue) to mess & Jean, Portner & I started to walk to show. Got picked up with a jeep & he rode us ½ way up a cliff & we went to central mess & then saw "Commandos" at #1 then went to grill & came home in cab with 2 cute drunk boys.

January 28, Thursday, 1943

Had a 9:30-3 off. Went to PX with Jean & Bernard & then visited Wilson & Bell on 111. Worked till 8:30 on 128-129-130-131 & walked over with Lt. Haas & we talked about General & Western Hills etc. Came in & wrote letters with Jean & Port. Had fun. Conley thinks he'll be back soon.

January 29, Friday, 1943

Was off at 3pm. Jean, Portner & I went to mess together & then went to show over near OCS & saw Andy Hardy then went to grill where I met a Sgt. I'd met on 138 cons with Gus, who wanted to take us out but we came home & shopped in the reck hall.

January 30, Saturday, 1943

Worked till 7. Had fun with Sgt. Miller, Cord & Marks. All the patients are cute. Jean & I were going with 2 other kids on a blind date but they never showed up so we stayed home & danced & stuff & had fun.

January 31, Sunday, 1943

Day of days. Overslept so I couldn't go to church. Worked 12:30-7.
Sgts. DeLucia, Rymer & the bunch were down. Sgt. Belinski (pt) played
guitar & tapped & we had a regular song fest. Conley came back about
3pm & then came up on the Ward about 6:30. I met him at 8pm & we
went over near OCS & saw "Commandos" again. It rained & we walked.

MEMORANDA

Month certainly ended up with a bang with the boys coming home from
Staten Island. Sgt. DeLucia called me up & told me to look out the back
of the Ward and I'd see him. So I ran down the back steps & he jumped
over the romp. It was wonderful.

February 1, Monday, 1943

Worked 7-11 & 3-7. Bill Mauer Cpl. Is one of my Ward men now.
Was debating whether to go to party at NCO club with Sgt. Gulman
& decided otherwise. Had fun on duty as per usual. Met Conley & Bill
Mauer & Welsch & myself went to theater #4 and saw double feature.
Came in early.

February 2, Tuesday, 1943

Worked 7-9:30. Stopped in harp PX then went up main PX & cashed my
check & met Jean & Port. Went & had permanents in the grill & we ate
lunch then went on duty 3-7 on 131 & Eisler Cpl. was a new Ward man.
It seemed funny that's he's with me again. Gulman called me then went to
work on 139 with Zimmerman & Deterra & gang. Conley called up there
but I stayed home & washed etc. Called home. Mom isn't feeling good.

February 3, Wednesday, 1943

Had a 3 off. Had fun on duty. Slept in afternoon & then went to gas
mask movie in Red Cross with Rymer & I lasted until 9pm & Rymer & I
hurt. Rushed to get dressed, we had dates at 9pm. She & her date, a Sgt.
rode us over to the OC & we saw "Shadows of Doubt". It was very good
& Conley was especially sweet.

February 4, Thursday, 1943

Had a 9:30-3 off. Went to commissary & central mess with Jean & Port & then we went to the grill for dinner. Went on duty at 3pm & had fun with patients especially Sgt. Miller. Then had to go relieve on 139 with Zimmerman & gang. Came off duty & washed etc. Had a picture in the paper of a tank they named after "Alabaster" who was killed.

February 5, Friday, 1943

Worked 7-3. Had the usual good time on duty. Met Conley at 8:30 & we walked to the show and saw "That Powers Girl." Felt closer to him and liked him better than I ever did before. Wish I really knew how I felt.

February 6, Saturday, 1943

Had a PM. Bill is back from his 3-day leave & we had fun, he, Eisler & I during inspection. Slept and messed around in the afternoon & wore Jean's winter outfit & we went to the show at OCA & I couldn't get in then went to #47 sat behind Col. & Major. Then went to service club & they closed it. The sneaking around gripes me. Wish we were in civilian life.

February 7, Sunday, 1943

Worked 7-12:30. Had a nice time on Ward with patients. Came off duty & slept. Went to show OCS with Conley & saw "Casblanca" again cause we didn't see much last night.

February 8, Monday, 1943

Worked 7-3. Went to Louisville with Portner & bought stuff for all patients & we ate Canary Cottage & went to show then came home on bus. Conley took Corp. Ex. today. Here's hoping.

February 9, Tuesday, 1943

Worked split. Had a 9:30-3 off & slept most of the time. Worked on split 130-131. Went on double date with Conley, Bill & Welch to show & saw "That Powers Girl." We went in cab. Conley made T/O. I was so tickled.

February 10, Wednesday, 1943

Had a 9-12:30 off. Had fun on duty. Mom is still sick. Went to Red Cross party given by Miss Hart with Jean & Tippie & Brown & Kramer. I went with Lt. Anderson, whom was very sick. We played ping pong & had our pictures taken.

February 11, Thursday, 1943

Worked split a 9:30-3 off. Sgt. Miller was discharged. We went up to PX & I bought different presents to send home etc. & wrapped them. Worked on 128-29-30-31 till 8:30 then went on double date with Conley, Bill & Welch to OCS show & saw "The Crystal Ball." I told him we just couldn't go together anymore because it was too dangerous. He took it swell.

February 12, Friday, 1943

Had a PM. Have 6 Ward men. Bill & Eisler included. Nice time on Ward. Jean's family were down. Rode into Louisville with them & we went to see "Random Harvest." It was wonderful. Ate in Canary Cottage & came home on bus – just Jean & I. Aunt Erna called long distance.

February 13, Saturday, 1943

Worked 7-3. Had inspection. Sandy Goodman was inspector. Aunt Erna & Jean came about 4pm & I called Slater. We made a room reservation for them & then went to #1 theater. Then went to the grill. Took Aunt Erna home in car & came home myself. Cute cab driver asked me for a date. Slater was very nice.

February 14, Sunday, 1943

It was very cold. Slept till 8. Aunt Erna & Jean came over then we went & met Slater & we all went to church in Red Cross then I took them down on the floor to visit & then to mess & Slater rode with them to Louisville. I went on duty 12-7 & then to #14 & saw "Immortal Sgt." With Port & Knight then to grill.

February 15, Monday, 1943

Had a 9-12:30 off because Bean was going on night. Got a card from
Conley. He went home on a 3-day pass & stayed in last night & caught
up with some work.

February 16, Tuesday, 1943

Worked 7-9 on 131 & 9-12:30 on 141 while patient Dissus moved on,
thinks he's a dog & climbs windows, doors etc. Then went down on 131
& worked till 3. A lot of new patients. Stayed in and washed, read, etc.
Conley called me this morning.

February 17, Wednesday, 1943

Had a 11-3 off. Stayed in and washed & stuff then went on 3-7. DeLucia
and Gulman told me they were going to OCS etc. Conley called &
wanted me to go to the show with him but I went with Jean, Rymer &
Knight and we saw "In Which We Serve." Then went to the grill.

February 18, Thursday, 1943

Had a PM. Miss Sparks gave Jean & I both notice of our leaves for the
23rd. Stayed in and packed my trunk & got things ready. Payton called
to say goodbye & DeLucia called. I called home and told them.

February 19, Friday, 1943

Had a 9-12:30 off. Had fun on duty as usual. Told Gulman & DeLucia
I was leaving & they rushed up to say goodbye but they knew I was
kidding. Conley called & I made a date for 9pm & we went for a walk. I
was in uniform & he was wonderful.

February 20, Saturday, 1943

Had a 7-3 off. Had fun on duty. Think we got another superior. Bill is
swell to work with & good too. Stayed in and washed & sorted things
to get ready for my leave. Conley called & so did Payton & Gulman.
Gulman called to say goodbye. He's going to Louisiana for a couple days.

February 21, Sunday, 1943

Worked 7-12. Not busy at all. Bill came on late & so did Lt. Moses.
He's cute, so nice & fun. Letter from home said Rhodes died day before
yesterday. Stayed in in the afternoon. Went for a walk with Conley for
about 1 ½ & said goodbye.

February 22, Monday, 1943

Worked 7-11 & 3-7. Had fun on duty. Got off at 11 and visited Jean
then she & I went up to the PX & ate & shopped & signed out @
headquarters. Went on duty 3-7 & had an especially good time with Bill
& DeLucia, patient Marks & Murdock. Saying goodbye to them all. I
got packed & ready to leave @ 12.

February 23, Tuesday, 1943

Ate at grill & then Jean & I got the 1:40 bus for Louisville & then the
2:40 train with some nice soldiers, one cute one who used my telephone
that I knew from 131. Took yellow cab home & got home at 8:30am.
Messed around all day & then went to Ruth & John's & then Weiss &
Hoff's came over from across the street.

February 24, Wednesday, 1943

Slept long. Ruth May stayed home from school. We went to Aunt Erna's
for dinner & saw everybody along the way. Met Stermer & went to Dr.
Hadkins chiropodist & then met Portner, her sister in-law, Kitty-Jean's
friend, Rosie B. Bergman, Betty & Ginny & went to the patio & saw
show & had chicken. Billy came in to say goodbye and we went to see
"Random House" again. Jean brought us home.

February 25, Thursday, 1943

Slept long. Went down to Grandpa's for dinner with Elinor & Marian.
Played piano etc. Then went to Grandma Reuter's for supper. Anna
Hartsmeyer was there. Uncle Bill brought out all his stuff from the last
war. Got a letter from Conley & one from Marks with pictures.

February 26, Friday, 1943

Slept late & then went with Ruth May & saw Miss Seg & all the kids. We went to see "Star Spangled Rhythm" with Mom, Dad & Ruth May. Stopped at Roaners on way back. Got a card from DeLucia in PA.

February 27, Saturday, 1943

Slept late. Gave mom, Ruth May & I each a facial. Rode to Aunt Erna's & then Jean & Uncle Charlie with us to Kit & Charles new home for Bonnie's birthday. We went up in the car. She was darling 1 yr. old. Elinor & Aunt Etta came. They had a farewell party for Dick at Aunt Freda's.

February 28, Sunday, 1943

Went to church which was crowded. Went to aunt's in the afternoon. Then Anna took Aunt Geneva to chicken supper on North Bend Rd. It was delicious. Ruth May & I went to Western Hills Church of Christ to hear Alma sing & then she came home with us for a while & stayed at her gramma's.

March 1, Monday, 1943

Slept long then got ready to go. Daddy came after us & I got the 10 min. to 6 bus. Felt kind of choked up when the bus pulled out. Had fun on the bus with with soldiers, one is coming to OCS @ Knox & took my name. Then had fun coming in taxi from stat. It pulled up with 5 boys in it & then we took them to Wasas wreck hall & then I had a ride with real cute driver who knew Carter.

March 2, Tuesday, 1943

1st day back on duty. Went to work on 150 with Newman & Maj. Sharp. Good to be back on duty & see all the kids. Conley & Gulman & all called. Met Conley @ 9 pm. It was slippery, cold & snowy & I fell & hurt my arm. We walked to OCS & saw a double feature and then walked back.

March 3, Wednesday, 1943

Went on duty for a while & then had to go to office to see Maj. Fisher & had an x-ray & he put on a splint. I was admitted on 111. Sgt. Gulman & DeLucia came & brought a bunch of stuff. Jean bought me everything.

March 4, Thursday, 1943

Had to be moved in another room for measure & we were so noisy. Had fun with patients. Got a note from Conley & one from Haybe. Wrote a letter home. A lot of the kids came over, Gulman & the other boys.

March 5, Friday, 1943

Had an infected finger & had it soaked & incised & pus taken out. Went to Orth & met Conley & he had an infected hand. Kids came up to visit. DeLucia, Koch called up. Reading "Frenchman's Creek" book of the month.

March 6, Saturday, 1943

Snowed again. Had inspection. Read etc. Rymer came up for a while. Sgts. Gulman & Koch came up & we visited on S. porch. Sgt. Naybar called up. Jean went in on 52 with measles. I talked to Conley on phone. Billie & Knight came over.

March 7, Sunday, 1943

Messed around & read etc. in morning. Then in afternoon Rollner, Donnelly & I went out on 3 hour pass. Went on 131 & 128 to visit kids & then went to PX & saw another bunch. Went to visit Jean & Maj. Gustafson on 52.

March 8, Monday, 1943

Read & messed around after taking a shower. Went to stage show & R.C. with Ralleri & on the way met Conley with a bunch of boys on the ramp. Some gave me a card from him, met all the boys at the show which was very good. Miller & Card came and sat next to us. Miller has his commission now but has to come back to 131 to commence.

March 9, Tuesday, 1943

Messed around, reading etc. Wrote 6 letters. Got a lot of mail including a darling birthday card from Gulmon. Called Jean up & talked to her. Ralleri was sent to 52 with measles after Lt. Peabody saw her.

March 10, Wednesday, 1943

Had a long talk with Naybar & decided to break off with Conley but I hated it. In the afternoon Col. Thomas had them move the measles on the Ward. Steamer & Ralleri. Sgt. Gulmon & Sgt. Miller phoned. Got a plant & notes from Rymer. Went to show myself @ R.C. Met patients of mine but sat upstairs with R.C. workers & then went to visit on 131 & was talking to Deterra. Had another phone call in evening but didn't know who from.

March 11, Thursday, 1943

Finished my book. Wrote letters. Messed around all afternoon. Called home long distance. In evening went to R.C. to see "Mad Medics" put on for doctors and nurses. It was cute. Put on by the 148th corp. enlisted men.

March 12, Friday, 1943

Messed around all day. Nothing unusual. In evening went to movie and saw "Forest Rangers." Sat in balcony with cute officers from 127. Then going out & DeLucia & kids stopped me & I was on romp & these 2 cute officers waited for me & wanted me to go to 127 & called me by name. And then went to medics party in wreck hall on pass. Got a birthday card from DeLucia.

March 13, Saturday, 1943

Messed around all morning & then had a pass signed by Lt. Miller. Walked to commissary & then to personal & filed income tax. Then went to central mess & signed up for family & then to P.O. & to beauty parlor. Had my hair washed & set. Walked home. Messed around area on pass in evening to quarters etc.

March 14, Sunday, 1943

Went to church & met Lt. Childers & Lt. Harris again & sat between them. They are really nice & friendly. Kidded with me all the time. They walked me down to 111 & knew all about Conley & everything. Got a letter from Marks. Sgt. Gulmon & DeLucia came to visit & then Betty Suppert & another girl from Borman Field brought me a book & we messed around in the evening.

March 15, Monday, 1943

Nothing unusual happened. Stayed in and read etc. In evening went to stage show put on by 1550. Went with Marks & sat with R.O. workers in balcony. Then went down on 139 to visit Deterra & Zimmerman & Wilson made rounds & told us to leave. Saw DeLucia about 9:30 when he made rounds on our floor.

March 16, Tuesday, 1943

Swell birthday. Got a big birthday cake from Ward. Had pass 1-9. Met family at bus station in rain. Then ate @ grill & then settled them at central mess. Took them to the PX & then to bowling alley. Ate at PX coffee shop. Back to central mess & then to #1 & saw "Frankenstein." Had fun with Lts. Had chocolate nut sundae at central mess & they walked me home. Got home on 111 & kids had my room filled with flowers & cards.

March 17, Wednesday, 1943

Family came after me on the Ward. Conley met us & was talking. Checked out central mess & ate at the cafeteria. Walked to PX country club library & watched them drill & OCS then went to bowling alley. Had a sandwich @ the grill. Put family on bus, came back to the Ward then went to movie at the RC. Didn't stay because I'd seen it. I came back on Ward. Bill called & said I should do something about Conley. Gulmon & DeLucia & another girl came over to ask me in evening. I went to see Jean & Conley called & said their Cadre is leaving.

March 18, Thursday, 1943

Read & wrote letters. Jean came over in the afternoon. Got another letter from Marks among others. In the evening Sgts Gulmon, Koch & DeLucia came over for awhile & we had fun. Then they went to NCO club & bought cheeseburgers & stayed till 11:00 pm.

March 19, Friday, 1943

Messed around all day, reading etc. Went to the show @ RC. Darling movie. Ginger Rogers & Cary Grant. Sat in balcony. When I came back to Ward Gulmon, Koch & DeLucia were there. They are swell kids. Walked with them to the romp & got my suit case. Went to bed early.

March 20, Saturday, 1943

Gulmon & DeLucia came over to visit and take pictures. Conley called up about noon. Saw the whole gang march off, 88 of them. Conley, Koch, Sgt. Schneider etc. It was awful again. Got a card from Holm & a letter from George wanting me to come home on leave. Gulmon & DeLucia were back in evening & we danced to the hit parade.

March 21, Sunday, 1943

Went to church & sat with the Lts. again. Bill was there & I was talking to him. Then walked with them down to 124 to see Sterner. After dinner went on pass from 1-9. Went to matinee @ #1 & saw "The Moon is Down" with Sterner, Conley & Portner & then we went to grill for supper. Came back to quarters & then Rymer came back with me. Gulmon & DeLucia were over for a while & we had cheeseburgers & cakes.

March 22, Monday, 1943

Read & wrote letters. Went to USO all girl show @ RC on The Old Side with Marks. It was good. Came over to PX & met Sgt. Gautlid & talked for a while & met Zimmerman in RC. Someone sent me baby oil through the mail. Gulmon & DeLucia called me & then came over & messed around till 10 pm.

March 23, Tuesday, 1943

Read in morning. Was going to RC show again but it was cancelled. Met the Lts. from 127 & we met Lt. McMan & Maj. Poole & one asked them if we couldn't go to club. Then we went to the RC & watched ping pong etc. Read in library. In evening DeLucia & Gulmon were up again for a while.

March 24, Wednesday, 1943

Read "Turning Leaves" all day. Maj. Sharp came back. Received another letter from Marks. In evening went to show – comedy. The Lts. were arguing on which side I should sit. I think Lt. Childers is cute. I could go for him. He's probably married. Sgts. Gulmon & DeLucia were over again. Nothing unusual happened.

March 25, Thursday, 1943

Finished book & got all set. Thought I was going to get discharged tomorrow. Went up & had my hair fixed. Went to quarters & got into uniform & went to mess with the kids over there. They had a farewell party for Col. Von Hook in wreck hall. Went on 141 with Sterner as she went on ND.

March 26, Friday, 1943

Was all set to go on duty & Maj. Sharp said he didn't have my chart fixed yet so I had to stay. Read & messed around. In evening went to RC show & saw "Casablanca." Sat next to Lt. Childers this time then went up & visited Jean. Helped on Ward when I got back. EdWards has measles now too.

March 27, Saturday, 1943

Got out this morning & went to work on 138. Nass-Agie is Ward man. Worked 8-11 & 2-7. Had inspection. Seemed wonderful to be on duty again. Bill was down & saw DeLucia. Zimmerman & Contrell were over. Kids all stayed in our quarters tonight. Gulmon called me.

March 28, Sunday, 1943

Went to church & Sgt. Gulmon & Lt. Haus were both there. Worked 12-7 on the Ward. Nothing unusual. Good time with pts. & DeLucia & Gulmon. Rymer asked me to go on double date with her. I went & we went to country club & then to Murphy's. He was strictly a wolf but I danced with another nice Lt. Didn't have a good time.

March 29, Monday, 1943

Worked 7-3. Had a nice time on Ward. Maj. Davidson is new Ward surg. Went to PX & had malted milk with DeLucia & Jon & kids. Then went to main PX & grill to see "Air Corps." Then went to Officers club & was talking to Lt. Bonested. Got an air mail letter from Conley & a card from Sgt. Koch. They're in California.

March 30, Tuesday, 1943

Had a 10-2 off & slept in afternoon. Gulmon came up & gave me his picture. The notice is up that I'm going on nights again 33-34-35. Was messing around on romp with Gulmon, DeLucia & some other Sgts., giving me pennies etc. & then Lt. Haus came up. He looked wonderful in uniform. Jean called and insists that I go with Rex.

March 31, Wednesday, 1943

Had a PM. Worked 7-12. Had a nice time on the Ward. Then Portner & I went to Louisville. Went to Leny's & shopped around then ate supper @ The Canary Cottage & then went to show & saw "Keeper of the Flame." Had cookies from DE, air mail from Conley & several other letters.

April 1, Thursday, 1943

Worked 7-12. Sort of hated to leave 138. Nice Ward. Came over & slept for a couple of hours. Then got up & ate supper & went on night duty. 33-34-35. Had Marks, Lannon & several other pts. I used to know. DeLucia brought sandwiches & kids all called up including Gulmon. 1st night wasn't so bad.

April 2, Friday, 1943

Slept all day then went to supper & then on duty. Nothing unusual happened. Have nice Wards and cute patients. Kids brought sandwiches from NCO club again & called up all night. Read and wrote letters etc.

April 3, Saturday, 1943

Went to breakfast then to bed & then got up & went to PX with Rymer & Jean. Met Sgt. Gulmon, DeLucia, Miller & Manion. They wanted us to go to ball game in Louisville tomorrow. Cincinnati Reds. One of the pts. uncle died & his CO, a Lt. was phoning about it & we had conversation. Said he'd call back. Brought sandwiches from NCO club again.

April 4, Sunday, 1943

Didn't go to church or ball game with the kids but got up & went to the matinee with a bunch of the AD kids. Came home & went to mess & then on duty. Had fun with pts. DeLucia & Rymer. Nothing unusual happened.

April 5, Monday, 1943

Got letter from Zimmerman. He's at Nichols. Nothing unusual happened. Usual good time on duty.

April 6, Tuesday, 1943

Got letter from Don & several others. Nothing unusual happened.

April 7, Wednesday, 1943

Had to get up early & go to drill. Had fun on duty. Lt. Bisslefield (old pt.) called over in quarters but I told him I was on nights. He is divorced now. Gulmon & friend came up for a while & then DeLucia. They all stayed until Marks had a spell. Got a letter from Don.

April 8, Thursday, 1943

Slept all day. Had 6 Wards because of meeting of 1 & 5. Had 30-31-32 along with mine. Was very busy. Capt. Gordmon was on his Wards. Had Capt. Williams look at sev. pts. Gulmon called & so did all the other kids. Nothing unusual happened. Got cookies from Marks that Ruth May sent.

April 9, Friday, 1943

Got up and went to commissary & around then paid bills. Came back & went on duty. Gulmon called & had usual good time with patients.

April 10, Saturday, 1943

Slept late and then went to mess & then on duty. Nothing unusual happened but Nabor told me Gulmon was restricted & no one could see him because he was leaving on a cadre & may be gone. It set me panicky, so I wrote him a note.

April 11, Sunday, 1943

Went to church & then to bed. Just as soon as I got on duty, Gulmon called & said they were only kidding me. Then a little while later he came up & stayed for a long while. Kids from A&D office came up & talked & night just flew.

April 12, Monday, 1943

Had fun with pts. etc. Then when we came off duty, Sparks called all the 80th together & told us we're leaving Wednesday. Then there was a fire drill & me and kids all went up and packed & messed around gathering things ready in the quarters. Talked to DeLucia. Finally packed my things and wrote home. Lennon and Marks kissed me goodbye. Relieved of night duty.

April 13, Tuesday, 1943

Went to work on H-20 with Wilson & Kramer until 12. Sneller & cutest bunch of boys we ever had. They were wonderful. Then went with kids to clear the post. Then had dinner & the country club with father of our gang. Goodman took & brought us home. He kissed me several times just to be funny. Went over on Rymer's Ward & kissed & said goodbye to him then went to Red Cross, Portner, & Gulmon & DeLucia called ½ dozen times & went to see them again & we went to 141 & we met Nabor & other kids. There was party in RC for us but we didn't stay. Called home twice long distance.

April 14, Wednesday, 1943

Had to be at Sparks office @ 8 am & then went to sign out. Said goodbye to everyone. Col. Morris, Schilling etc. Then got ready after going to little PX to visit kids. Train left at 4 pm. Gulmon & DeLucia even came to the station. Had private lunch & stay over in Louisville, all 15 of us @ the French Village.

April 15, Thursday, 1943

Got up and went to breakfast at diner. Then arrived at Montgomery at 10:30 am & had lay over. Messed around shopping, ate dinner ate hotel then to show. Had to be back on train at 6:30. Had to take regular train & was full of the most polite, cute sailors & we sang & talked & joked. When we arrived @ Ozark about 10, they helped us out & wished us luck.

Mt. Sinai, New York

April 16, Friday, 1943

Had breakfast. Then signed up & got helmet, bed rail & all equipment & signed up at finance & went to headquarters about 10-12 times in all to get all set. Had fun up there. Big office & they gave us cookies & then took us to the large mess hall & we had cookies & coffee. Went to PX, had sundaes & bought stuff. It's big & crowded. Had several meetings throughout the day. Stayed in headquarters till 5am & met 3 Cinti boys.

April 17, Saturday, 1943

Got tetanus shots. Got to see pictures. Went to PX & bought more stuff. Didn't sleep much, even took mattresses out from under us.

April 18, Sunday, 1943

Slept & had fun singing – rain. They sure do give us the food.

April 19, Monday, 1943

Train. Rain. 6:15 good supper. Wonderful clean-up after being so dirty & comfortable beds are swell. All the kids are swell and I think we're really going to have fun.

April 20, Tuesday, 1943

Got up and had a swell breakfast. At noon we were calmly eating dinner & in walked Jean, Rymer, Kramer & all the kids we really had a shock reunion & then to top it off we met another group of kids. Had general inspection this afternoon then went to PX. Came back & washed after supper & washed hair. Then the adjustment etc. came over.

April 21, Wednesday, 1943

Overslept & was hauled out because we were late. McCabe is now my roommate since we've been here. Browning was @ the other place. Capt. Chamberlain & all are nice. Had our gas masks checked this afternoon & had our typhus shots. We all walked to the dispensary. Capt. Klein gave us a lecture & Greensburg (Warrant officer) had us fill out more cards.

April 22, Thursday, 1943

Had another full field inspection. Signed some papers & walked miles & everyone went through gas chamber. Then another meeting & some of the kids got to go to NG McCabe brought me a new sentence from the main officer's store. Browning & kids went to the PX which we packed & then met 5 Lts. who took us to the show. Some cute kids.

April 23, Friday, 1943

Got more jeans & then went to quarters in a truck & bought fatigues & long underwear etc. Then had lunch & got all GI issue again. Then went to dentist. 2 civilians gave us a ride up. He said my teeth were bad and blamed too much brushing. Came back & got ready to go to NYC & the trip was cancelled. Had 8 letters including one from George & Marks. Went to show again. Then heard Red Cross calling Jean & went to find her in barracks.

April 24, Saturday, 1943

Got more mail from home & my beige suit came. Laid around and slept all day & finally got to go to a small PX just for nurses. We're restricted just to one area because of paratroopers being so wild. Nothing unusual happened. Packed again & went to see Jean & kids several times.

April 25, Sunday, 1943

Got up & took bath & then to church & it was packed with enlisted men, officers, nurses alike. We stayed for communion, it was beautiful. Had another meeting & got 7 letters & answered a lot of them & then went to PX & saw movie "Wake Island." Very good but terrible.

April 26, Monday, 1943

In afternoon messed around & went over to see Sterner & then mail & then foot lockers came & we unpacked. Then went to double feature up at PX & then went over with kids again. Nothing unusual.

April 27, Tuesday, 1943

Had drill this morning. Up to the road & got another typhus shot this afternoon. Slightly depressed today. Nothing exciting. Felt better after I cleaned up & went to double feature with Roedes. Refined date to go to Col. Party @ the club. Bernard wanted me to go.

April 28, Wednesday, 1943

Got to go NYC on a 12 hour pass from 5 – 5 & went in on bus & crossed George Washington Bridge & got the subway. Then went to The Commodore Hotel & got tickets to see show & then went to nice restaurant & had steak supper but when walking to restaurant I heard someone yell "Arlene" & there was Bud Gionette. He's at some comp in NY. We talked for a couple of minutes then he took my address & I had to go with the kids. It was a wonderful feeling. Then the show was the funniest & best I have ever seen. Then went to drug store & kids called long distance then went to Crossroads. I had fun. Got on subway & got home to comp at 3 am.

April 29, Thursday, 1943

Everyone had to go out for drill. The other kids got to go to NY & we went to show. Mac & Cronley & I then asked some enlisted men to get us some sandwiches @ the PX but they couldn't get any. There was bottle boys gave us sandwiches, cakes & everything.

April 30, Friday, 1943

Went to lecture & the station hospital by Julia Stimpson. Was supposed to triple date with Mac, Polkingham, Beused, Miller & myself with Pertella. The plans were messed up so I went in with other kids on the bus & the enlisted men & we sang on the way in. Then as the RC workers & kids were calling up we waited on a corner @ the bus station. I noticed a crowd of officers across the street & they hollered at one. Left & took the subway to Time Square & then a taxi to the Commodore Hotel, sang all the way. Then Pertella & I went after the Theater tickets & came back & met the others & we had dinner at the hotel. Took a cab to the Empire & saw "Life with Father." Then into another cab & went to quarters. Had a swell time. Had a wonderful dinner & fun time at floor show, was the best any had ever seen. Good food & all the crowd was swell. Had our picture taken a couple of times.

May 1, Saturday, 1943

Messed around again all day & then tonight went to see "The Harmon Comedy." It was wonderful but sad. Came over & was going to write letters etc. but Lt. Pertella called & asked me to cross over to the club so I got dressed & went over for about 2 hours. We danced with the juke box etc. Fun. He acts nicer all the time, that's what worries me. That I'll like him much more. Then he'll like me. Another wonderful night.

May 2, Sunday, 1943

Went to church. Had a pass. 1pm & went in with Bernard. Went to Commodore Hotel & called home. Met Moe, Browning, Polky, Miller & Pertella walked in with date from Brooklyn. Ate at the Commodore & went shopping. Had a nice time Came home on the bus & got all ready fixed BB & BR for 5am. Had a letter from Marks.

May 3, Monday, 1943

Had physicals again. Got paid & then had to have new gas masks checked & then had to go through gas chamber again. Nothing unusual happened. Some of the boys went on ahead. Got a letter from Gulmon he's in the brig. Washed hair, fixed nails etc.

May 4, Tuesday, 1943

Packed & got ready. Heavy packs & helmets & everything & still the band played "A Pretty Girl is Like a Melody" for us. Then the Red Cross served doughnuts & coffee etc. Saw Lt. Pertella several times but not enough to talk to.

May 5, Wednesday, 1943

Beautiful day. Feel swell but did not sleep well last night. Met the Lt. on bow with Mac & Palky for a while. Wonderful experience so far. Very calm in evening, everyone went to Lounge.

May 6, Thursday, 1943

Had officers call in Lounge after breakfast. Good meals by the way.
Then went up on deck & got a good sunburn & had fun over on the side
with Owens & kids & several Lts. & then some Enlisteds came over &
we had a lot of fun comparing England with us. Was called to go to Cols.
Party, but didn't go.

May 7, Friday, 1943

Had to work 7-3. It was the most fun I've had. Worked on Surg Wd. &
slated out with 2 pts. Had ended up with several more & then transferred
some out. Rough day.

May 8, Saturday, 1943

Still having fine weather & good meals. In morning was up on deck with
Mac reading. In afternoon Lt. Risdell met Bernard & I and then she left
& we spent the afternoon up on deck. He was reading my magazine.
After supper in Lounge we had 2 orchestras & we had a swell time. It
was with him & others. We danced. I have a terrific sunburn.

May 9, Sunday, 1943

Slept till 9. Went to church & had a very nice service. Crowded. It was
thrilling at the end, sang "My Country, Tis of Thee." Spent the afternoon
with Lt. Benehart. He's very nice, attentive & fun. Sat on deck for a
while & then circulated all around avoiding this Maj. & Capt. In evening
had a swell time in lounge. Had a date with him again & we had a song
fest & music. We had an argument about going out on deck after he'd
fixed it with a Np after they closed the lounge we stayed out with the
enlisted & had another song fest. All the other kids like him too.

May 10, Monday, 1943

Had a nice breakfast & then had drill & went up on deck till noon.
Then came up & we were reading bout HQ. We layed out on deck all
afternoon. Then I visited him while he was on duty. Then met him to
go to medics party in the lounge which was a success. We talked to the
engineers on the ship again & Alfy, young Britain was going to take us
up on deck but the plans were muffed.

May 11, Tuesday, 1943

He met me this morning on deck & a gang of us played "I doubt it." Beautiful day again. Had a date on deck this afternoon again & Alfy saw the English officers were there for a while. Met him after supper & he helped me with my pack etc. then went up on deck & were there quite a while. The MPs didn't stay and then when he went in for his field jacket, Mac & all the others told me they were paging me over the loud speaker. Miss Chamberlain wanted me to go on duty so I rushed down. Went to work for a couple of hours & didn't have to work nights as planned so they put a call through for him & he came down for a while & left since we were busy. He came back again and we went out on deck then came in. He was cold. Then the English engineers invited me to their party & went down & had sandwiches. They have really been swell to us.

May 12, Wednesday, 1943

Had breakfast at 8 & then went on deck & Rinehart found me on the bow & we went out on the spot deck & had the biggest thrill ever watching all excitement together. He was very sweet & then we said good bye. There was a band again & everyone was so friendly. Finally settled in, very nice girls. Comfortable, clean. It's all beautiful and interesting.

Casablanca, Morocco

May 13, Thursday, 1943

Had a good night sleep & breakfast at 8:30 am. Came over and wrote letters & got fixed up & then had a very good dinner, steak etc. & there were some fellows from the Signal Corps over. Walked over to the other kid's quarters & then in the park across the street & several soldiers and sailors came up & we talked all afternoon. Had a good supper & the fellows brought over barrack bags & bed rails.

May 14, Friday, 1943

Had good meals all day. Didn't do anything special. Wrote letters & took a nice shower. Crowly moved in with me & Browning with Luhonovic. The weather is still balmy. Saw Lt. Jackson from Ord tonight. Went over in park for a while. We're still very much restricted.

May 15, Saturday, 1943

Had a sun bath with Mury in morning. After dinner went to park & met the soldiers in the park who had the hose for us. Then walked to town & shopped around. All the service men were so friendly. They even have a dept. store. Then after supper Rinehart called for me & rode us to town & we walked around & sat in the park. It was wonderful seeing him. He still has a bad cold & he was very sick. It was his first night out and it was wonderful seeing him again. We saw the sights & then he had a truck bring me home. I gave him asprin & cookies.

May 16, Sunday, 1943

Slept late. Had chicken for dinner. After dinner we went over in the park & wrote letters & talked to the soldiers & they let me have a ride on the French bike. I came over and Rinehart came about 3 instead of 5. I couldn't get ready in time & he had to go on & he had to be restricted but he came & we had a ride & then went to Sidewalk Café & then a restaurant & had a Spaniard walk us down to the park & we sat in the park for a while. Then all the officers from the Signal Corp took us home. Had a swell time & he is very sweet.

May 17, Monday, 1943

Slept long & Rinehart came & I had to get out of bed as we went for a walk & then sat and talked & then he had to go. Then went to dinner and on the way back there he was again @ 2pm & he was supposed to be OD from noon today til noon tomorrow. Then we went on duty and then went to a reception for the Surgeon General & they had orchestras, food & everything. Danced with Maj. Kline & shook hands with Surgeon General of the USA. Came home early.

May 18, Tuesday, 1943

Worked 8:30-1. Sewed cuffs on OR gowns & went through the hospital. Saw the Surg. Gen. again. Had something taken out of my eye in ENT clinic. Got it in the other night. Came home by bus & got dressed in beige. Rinehart came about 3 & we went down & went shopping & stopped in Allies Off. Club & another place & then came back for supper & when we started out again in his truck the Np's got, and no one responded & we had to walk. We walked around park & he told me all about his past life etc. then we kind of made up & then came home in truck again.

May 19, Wednesday, 1943

Worked 8:30-1 & then 2:30-5. Made gauze sponges & wrapped them & sewed glove cases on the machine. Met Lt. Zimov who is Lou Zimov's cousin. He is an MAC in the 66th & very nice. Talked about Cincy & met enlisted man from Cincy who knows all the kids I know & we really had a chat. It did us all good. Stayed home & washed & washed my hair & wrote letters and listened to the radio. I didn't hear from him today. I wonder what happened.

May 20, Thursday, 1943

Worked on the Wards today & met several Knox boys. In afternoon sewed on the machine again. Stayed home in the evening & he called but I didn't have much chance to talk. He's restricted for a week & says he'll be down as soon as he's out & that I shouldn't forget we're going steady.

May 21, Friday, 1943

Sort of a dull day. Worked downstairs in OR & then served trays on the
Wards. Did the same in the afternoon. They're all very nice, friendly
crowd. Got 4 letters. Could have had oodles of dates if we'd wanted them
but still wasn't in the mood. Took my blue dress to French woman with
Biggs & then wrote letters & listened to the radio.

May 22, Saturday, 1943

Worked in OR & Sgt. brought us pastries etc. In afternoon went to May
Festival & girls school. It was very good. In evening went to Air Corps
dance @ RC with Lt. whom I was introduced to by Roeder, went with
Sato & Bussard on trip date. Went to party. Tom Harmon, star football
player was there & we had a good lunch, ice cream.

May 23, Sunday, 1943

Worked on Ward again today. Had fun with patients & enlisted men.
Went to church in their chapel & the chaplain is wonderful. I was really
touched and thrilled. When I got home from work Rinehart had left a
message, he was coming @ 6:30 bus restriction was lifted so we triple
dated with Fuller, Porta & another couple. We had fun, started at the
Club & met everyone we know, then walked the streets for a while & met
several of their men. Then went to a nice restaurant for supper & then to
Mona's.

May 24, Monday, 1943

Had the day off. Slept long & washed. Rinehart was going to have the
day off too but he called at noon & said he couldn't but I should be ready
by 2:15 just in case he could come in & then he couldn't & so he called
at 4 and said he'd be in at 6:15 & then they had some special orders, so
some sgt. delivered a message through Beatz that if they went here by
8:30 they couldn't come & then at 8 he called and said he was terribly
sorry but the whole base was restricted. So I dressed and undressed all
day.

May 25, Tuesday, 1943

He came at 6:30 & we had a lot of fun just messing around downtown meeting everyone we know. Stopped in for ice cream, then went to R.C. movie & saw "Keeper of the Flame." Then walked home. Had fun walking home. He is so cute & sweet & very smart. When we were saying good night, he said he could tell me something but I would only laugh & not believe him but he would mean it anyway & then he shut up.

May 26, Wednesday, 1943

Worked for Red Cross all day & in the evening met Richard & Fuller at 6:30 for Porter & I. We had fun walking around & then we went out for supper & had fun. He got mad because I was always talking to enlisted men. Then we met Biggy & Roeder with their dates & we went to the ABS club and danced. Then we had to leave early & when we got home he told me he really loved me & would never forget me no matter what I said. He was very sweet & tried so hard to convince me but I couldn't believe it.

May 27, Thursday, 1943

Worked on the balcony in Ward but didn't work hard, got a letter from Portner. Took all but 10 patients down in balc. & had fun with them. In the evening, Rinehart & Clark came for Biggy & I & before we were even out of the grounds he reminded me of what he said the night before & that he was saying it in the daylight. We stopped several places to eat & had fun meeting everyone we knew along the streets & then we went to the opening of the Ox & saw the "Sea Hawk." He was wonderful again & just as we were saying good night he was telling me he really meant it. They played "Taps" and we both cried.

May 28, Friday, 1943

Discharged all patients from balc. & took all equipment back to med. Supply & then had a good dinner. In afternoon did PX shopping for the patients in the PX & had a lot of fun. Worked pretty hard. Talked to the fellows in the PX for a while & then had a coffee with Lt. Rymer & some others. They're very nice. Reinhart was OD. Stayed home & washed hair & clothes, etc.

May 29, Saturday, 1943

Had fun on duty talking to paratroopers etc. Ate over there & got off at
2:30 & got a ride home with Lts. Palky, Miller & Price. Washed & got
things straightened out & he was supposed to come at 6:30 and didn't
get here until 7:30 because of a meeting. We walked downtown & went
and saw Deanna Durbins "First Love". It was very good. We had a sort
of misunderstanding about things and & almost broke up all together.
I have a feeling we will soon. He says he'll try and come in today but I
doubt it so I'm going out anyhow.

May 30, Sunday, 1943

Had a PM and went to church in morning. It was very good. I didn't
know it was coming but at 1 there he comes strolling in. We went to
the park across the street & he was so tired. I let him sleep for a while,
& then we walked downtown & had supper & then walked around &
watched a ball game & listened to a band concert in the park. Then we
planned how we'd live & what we'd do when & if we got married. Had
fun. Then we went to the show again & had lounge seats in the front
row with several other Signal Corp fellows & saw everyone we knew &
walked home.

May 31, Monday, 1943

Worked on the same Ward. Had a PM & went to town and bought some
more stuff. Got ice cream cones & a ride home and then ironed & washed
& cleaned up the place. After supper we had to go through the chamber
across the street. Stayed in house, he had officers meeting & washed &
then the kids were all playing with my hair & giving me a new hairdo.

MEMORANDA

This has been truly the most wonderful month I ever spent in my life or
ever intend to spend. Seeing this romantic city with the swellest guy in
the world who intends to marry me.

June 1, Tuesday, 1943

Had fun on duty. Wrote letters. Wasn't busy. In the evening, he came & said he would try to come back in a half hour. He did & we went to the Petit Ponchet & had omelets, sat at the same table with Walt Bodenburg & then met everyone we knew. We had fun making plans again.

June 2, Wednesday, 1943

Worked in Plaster room & had fun with the sgts. Nothing unusual happened. He called & said he had the ring & would try and get in if he didn't have to go to this special meeting but he had to & didn't get in at all. I stayed in & talked to the kids.

June 3, Thursday, 1943

Worked in Plaster room again & had oodles of fun arguing with one of the fellows especially. They brought us candy, mints & lemonade. He couldn't come in again because they did some construction work.

June 4, Friday, 1943

Worked in the Orth. room all day & the boys brought us candy etc. One of the sgts. asked me to go with him & another one to go with Biggy. Had a PM & went down shopping, had ice in the Florian. Met a lot of officers I knew from Orth. Went to bank and changed money & came home in horse cab. He came in about 7:15, put the ring on the right finger to stay & we had ice cream with a Sgt. & French girl & then went to movie with Bailey & Red & they had a community sing. He showed Red my ring & then turned it around. Was very sweet but is leaving tomorrow morning on a job at 7:30 am.

June 5, Saturday, 1943

He left at 7:30 am this morning to go out on construction job. Had fun planning on taking trip out to see him. One of Crowley's pts. knew how to get there. Had fun with Major Phillips & all the fellows in the Plaster room. Stayed home & wrote letters & washed etc.

June 6, Sunday, 1943

Slept long. Decided not to go see him because we had to be back at 1:00 to go on duty even though the bus left & we had to come back. Then we got there & there wasn't anything to do so some of us left and took a carriage home. Washed my hair etc. Stayed in again & when Biggy came in & told me Clark told her he was expecting me this afternoon.

June 7, Monday, 1943

Made plaster again all morning & had fun with the boys. When we came home @ lunch he was here in jeep with a pnt. & Doubletime, it was wonderful to see him again & we talked for a while then he walked me in to dinner. In afternoon Morgan took my address etc. & said he will be here in Cincy. In evening 3rd General had a party in our wreck hall but we didn't go. They did bring us sandwiches.

June 8, Tuesday, 1943

Slept through breakfast. Got all packed & washed clothes & got everything set to move tomorrow. Didn't get to see him @ all today. All officers are restricted for 24 hours because their places are not strictly GI.

June 9, Wednesday, 1943

Had to be packed by 8:00. Sat around & wrote letters & had fun doing the polka with Henry & her harmonica. Got 3 air mail letters, one from Ruth May telling me about DeLucia coming to Cincinnati & they really had a swell time. I'm so glad we came out on trucks & really had a swell time fixing up our tents. Had a wonderful meal in a clean mess hall & we really like it. It's fun, we're going to be healthy.

June 10, Thursday, 1943

Had a very good breakfast & then messed around all day fixing up our tents etc. Had a letter from DeLucia & he said he was planning on going to Cincy. Nothing unusual. Still restricted. Bob was up & tried to get in but the guards chased him away, so he gave a note to Lt. Ballard to give to me.

June 11, Friday, 1943

Wrote letters in the wreck hall. We're still restricted. Bob came down & I
got to talk to him for a while, it was swell to see him again, he had a note
written for me & then came back in for about 2 hours with another note.

June 12, Saturday, 1943

Was CQ 8-12:30. Was busy & swept the floor & had inspection. The
restriction was lifted @ noon but he didn't come in so I stayed in in the
afternoon. Then he came about 7:00 after I changed with "Blitzate" but
I went anyhow because he came the 30 miles & had a flat along the way.
He gave me a flashlight with his name on it & then went jeep riding &
got ice cream & then rode along the ocean.

June 13, Sunday, 1943

Went to church & then right after dinner we went to Fedula beach with
Raeder, Bensle & Lt. Stormy & all his gang. Had a swell time in the
ocean & on the beach. & then came home in a truck with all his enlisted
men & then they took pictures. Had a lot of fun but missed supper. Bob
was down this morning & told me about his accident & gave me his
note & was going to try & get in tonight but he came & couldn't wait to
see me because of the restriction & he had to go to a marshall & that he
couldn't see me anymore.

June 14, Monday, 1943

Had breakfast earlier & then calisthenics after which the Sgts. drilled us
& then we had lectures. Had Frankie cut my hair & set it after I washed
& showered. Called Bob after supper & he sounded awfully disgusted
but said he'd write & I feel so sorry and awful for him. I wrote him a
letter & driver took it down for me.

June 15, Tuesday, 1943

Had calisthenics, drill etc. & the classes. Got 2 letters, one from DeLucia
and one from Betty. Messed around all day & in evening went down to
the men's quarters & they had a GI show for us which was very good.
Pres. was master of ceremonies. It was fun sitting just any old place.
Came home & wrote Bob a letter.

June 16, Wednesday, 1943

Had calisthenics & drill then classes. Received 8 letters from home, Alma
& Zimmerman. Bob sent up a darling sweet letter by Lt. Robertson &
then I wrote him one & sent it down with Lt. Gilbert. We had a colonel
band play for us & then we wrote letters. I feel so much better since I got
his letter & I know he loves me.

June 17, Thursday, 1943

Went on road march this am. It was fun. In afternoon went to town
on truck & did some small shopping. Bought him a coloring book for
silliness & to occupy him. Met 2 officers who took us to a café & then
walked to 6th gen. for truck. Insisted we go with them again. All the
fellows were friendly in town. Came home and had letters from Gulman
& DeLucia & another from Reinhardt. Wrote him and told him exactly
what I thought. Then went to outdoor movie and saw "The Road to
Morocco."

June 18, Friday, 1943

Had drill & classes. Nothing unusual happened. Went with 9 other kids
to a chicken supper. Wore beige suit & rode out in command car & we
ate up on roof. Then Lt. Seitz said he'd show me Camp DeShone so we
just jumped up from the table & he drove me there in jeep & was very
nice & we got Bob & left us to talk for a long time. He wanted us to stay
for the show or for me to & then go home with Betty but I didn't think
that would be nice so we stayed a long while then drove back just in
time to come back again & we came back in command car. It was a very
pleasant evening after all.

June 19, Saturday, 1943

Had inspection & then went down to inspect the men's area. It looked
nice. Didn't feel good all day. Had terrible cramp-like pains. Washed in
afternoon. We all stayed home in the evening & wrote letters etc. I still
didn't feel good.

June 20, Sunday, 1943

Felt sick all day. Didn't even go to church. Nothing unusual happened.
Stayed in & wrote letters & went to bed early.

June 21, Monday, 1943

Had drill practice for retreat & had class etc. Went to Tom's with
Betty on truck. Went to quartermates & bought a lot of stuff. Met the
officers that we met the other day, asked me for a date again. Left our
packages at the hospital. Went to a medics party at the Robinson hotel.
Had orchestra & food. Had pretty much fun with Zimon & Pertella but
Pertella got drunk & came home in a weapons carrier.

June 22, Tuesday, 1943

Practiced for the retreat & had classes. Washed & packed clothes. Lt.
Clark came about 7:00 & we went to town in Jeep. It was his first night
out again & we all had fun walking the streets & teasing back and forth.
Clark said they really teased him about me coming to see him with
another Lt. Stopped at a sidewalk café & then went to Vox movie. The
Sgt. met us & we came home in a Jeep again. Had fun & he was very
sweet.

June 23, Wednesday, 1943

Had drill & then the kids practiced. Got a lot more mail including a letter
from Sgt. Koch, Groman, Kit & some from home. Our party started
at 8:00 for the enlisted men. I wore DeWitt's darling formal & was a
hostess. The show was a big hit & the enlisted men sat in front & then
we danced on the stage. Had a good orchestra & we danced with all the
enlisted men. They had a wonderful time. I danced with a T/5 from Hq.
Then they had to go home & we changed & went and washed dishes &
did KP song & everyone came over there & we sang church songs & ate
cheese sandwiches & had lemonade.

June 24, Thursday, 1943

Called off retreat. Washed etc. I went to the PX. Bob came while I was
taking a shower to tell me he was in trouble & couldn't stay & that he'd
try & come back, but he couldn't. I called & he said I should meet him
in town in front of the P.O. I went with Biggy & Lt. Zimon & then met
him. Was he depressed and blue? They really have a case against him so
we talked & sat in the park & I tried to cheer him up. Then he couldn't
take me home because he didn't have a permit so we went up to the front
of the house and met Gelmeron & some others & we called a truck and
got home.

June 25, Friday, 1943

Folded gauze in the morning etc. Went to beach with Stormy & gang on truck & had fun. Washed my hair & stayed in. The Red Cross & Woves moved in. Nothing unusual. Didn't get to see Bob.

June 26, Saturday, 1943

Messed around all day. He came over early in the afternoon & we talked etc. & said he'd be over at 2:00 & we'd just mess around the camp. Then about 2 hours later he came back & said he couldn't come, so we sat in the Jeep & talked. He's trying to get transferred into our outfit. In evening went to a Repl. Dedication of their new club. Didn't like it. Linda & I had a driver take us downtown to the dance. We had a slightly better time and had ice cream & cake.

June 27, Sunday, 1943

Band played in morning & woke us up & went to church. Went to the beach with Alma, Stormy & Reinhardt met me there. We had a wonderful time. Met his whole crowd of his Off. He went home on the truck with us & then Alma & I ate at 701 Club & had a wonderful meal. Then came back & got dressed & Bob came with Lt. Monroe & I got him a date with Frankie. We had fun. Joined the auto club & danced and drank champagne. It made me feel kind of funny but they were all so nice to me. Then Monroe took Frankie home after we parked. Read funny sheets.

June 28, Monday, 1943

All the kids or rather most of them took the trip to Rabat. We stayed here & Bob came down in a Jeep while on the job & we talked for about an hour & then Alma took one picture with her camera & then Stormy came after us & we went to town in the afternoon & I met Bob in QM. Then we went back to work & Alma and I went to the matinee. & we had ice cream. Then we met Stormy & went shopping & then waited for Bob. Finally I called & Fuller said he'd already gone. I went back to the PO & there he was. We were supposed to wait for Biggy & Clark but they didn't come so we left the auto club & went and met Alma & Stormy for supper & then went to the AB Club & danced. Stormy had a weapons carrier & we came out to our camp & then went to Stormy's 701 club and had grilled cheese sandwiches. He was the sweetest he's ever been & I loved him more than ever.

June 29, Tuesday, 1943

They turned the water on again & we washed, ironed etc. Nothing unusual happened. Didn't get to see him & missed him very much.

June 30, Wednesday, 1943

Slept long and then worked all day. In the afternoon he sent a note up that they were again restricted. I called at 5:30 & he said he'd be out & so he sent Monroe over to take Brownie and myself to dinner @ La Reserve & we had a duck dinner overlooking the sea. Then went back to Du Shone & met Bob. He had to work till 9:15 pm & we saw the movie & then he had to pay some men. Then we went to the Sphinx & drank champagne & sang. Then went for a ride & got in at 3:00 am.

MEMORANDA

This has been one horrible and yet wonderful month. We both realized we truly love one another with all our hearts and yet it's been torture because of the constant restrictions and the conditions caused by the war itself. If only we could be married & be in civilian life.

July 1, Thursday, 1943

Packed barracks bag & slept in afternoon. Bob came in the afternoon & we sat out in the Jeep with 2 of his enlisted men. After he finished work he & Monroe came after Brownie & I and we rode into town but it was too late to do anything so we went out to the Sphinx & all the Signal Corps & all the kids were out there and had a nice time & then went for a ride. We almost had a really final fight but I think he was trying me out. We ended up with final vows & he gave me his insignia & put a ring on the right finger. I really love him more than anything in the world.

July 2, Friday, 1943

Did bed rolls etc. & the water finally came on & we took showers & I washed my hair. All we had to do was wait there at first. They thought we wouldn't be going because the French took over and then they settled & we did. Lt. Phillips told me to write Bob a note & he'd see that he got it but I gave it to Stormy because he was with us & brought the picture. He said he'd be sure he got it. Was terribly lonely for him. We left for Fez @ 7:30 am

July 3, Saturday, 1943

Really on our way. Stopped in town for breakfast & for lunch was looking, hoping & expecting Bob but was surprised & thrilled when I saw he & several of his officers walk out of the RR Station as we pulled into it. He had a real reunion with everyone. They arranged for trucks & dinner for all the nurses. Then Biggy, Brownie & Heeny went with us. He pulled us up to the Jeep & then they took us to their beautiful hotel & his room was so darling & comfortable. We were all going to take a bath and then they brought us down to the station & we said goodbye. He called up all the cities along the way & spent the whole day at the station waiting for me. He really convinced me he loves me & is going to miss me. It was wonderful.

July 4, Sunday, 1943

Had breakfast late & talked over yesterday with Heeny, especially Bob's hotel. Again in the early afternoon we stopped and had biscuits, corned beef & pickles. The scenery is gorgeous. We slept in the afternoon & arrived in Oujda in the evening. Had corned beef, cabbage & soup and had to wait hours and hours for water. The enlisted men & all mingled together & T/5 Stein finally got some water. All the boys were telling me what a jewel I had in Bob. They're crazy about him.

July 5, Monday, 1943

It was very misty & we had a larger breakfast than usual. The scenery was magnificent in the mountains & we were up in the clouds all morning. Had corned beef again for lunch & Red met Burley from Ord. Stopped at small town and had supper. It was much better too. Tried to call Jean but the line was always busy. Sent her a note with Capt. Jenning from Ord. Everyone was out for a couple of hours & there 2 French smart alecks asking a lot of questions. Didn't get to bed till late because the kids next door took so long to get settled. I miss Bob so much sometimes I could die.

July 6, Tuesday, 1943

Didn't stop for breakfast. Had breakfast & dinner combined. Met American troops from Oid & Signal. Had showers – heavenly & put on slacks. Passed several prisoner trains of Italians and Germans & another hospital train. Stopped for a good supper. Chile etc. & the train pulled out & left ½ of the train Col. included @ Mess. We went to the next town & waited for them. Then went back & picked them up. Threw flowers to them & sang "The med. Corps Went Over the Hill." Eddie Stack ran along the top of the cars & finally convinced the French to turn back. Then we met an Am. Troop train & had fun with them. Still miss Bob terribly.

July 7, Wednesday, 1943

Beautiful, in fact, gorgeous mountains. Had fun following truck convoy. Stopped several hours & talked to Eng. 8th army. One of them gave me a stallion ring & another an English cigarette. They were so cute & brave, just out of the hospital. We got hauled out for giving letters to EM to mail. Other kids got hauled out for mixing with EM & the officers got in trouble for getting EM on the train with a lot more liquor. Everyone was upset & they stopped the train & put the fellows off. Then after supper we had both am. Eng. and French Eng. & they couldn't get together so there was a fist fight about signals & we were stalled on a hill & couldn't get started & then we jumped so much everything came down on top of us.

July 8, Thursday, 1943

Peaceful fairly happy day. Good food. Large air party along the line. Trying fortresses in formation, it was very thrilling. Read, talked, Maj. Klein visited for a while & Capt. visited also, among others. Passed trains along the line & they had to detach us for a while & go back and get our boys & then were pulled up next to us for a while & we could talk. Capt. Schwartz came along. Was just wishing for something to eat. Was very hungry before going to bed. Almost hysterical.

July 9, Friday, 1943

Cool & rainy this am. Had a good breakfast with German prisoners just next to us. Had sandwiches for lunch. Beautiful country always. Met cute Americans from an Armed din & a lot of interesting country. Fo. Charles, bomb shells baled area, caused Messerschmitt alley a lot of German prison camps. Our boys stole a duck and by the time we arrived at the next station they had received a telegram & they came out and asked about it so Maj. Bick & Lt. Shea had Sgt. Dowd come tapering out with it & it was plucked & everything. They said it flew in & was stunned.

Mateur, Tunisia

July 10, Saturday, 1943

Arrived in early am & slept on train. Had breakfast @ the station & then came out to the camp & hospital in trucks. All of what we could see was bombed. Air field next to us & planes all over the place. Marshall's boyfriend is here. Just about got our stuff in our tents & had to go on duty & work like dogs not even having any rest or sleep or being able to wash. Did woodwork windows & everything. Worked till dark then set up lots & had to have someone move in with us. Wrote a letter by flashlight to Bob. Everyone is in & out. Men all over the place.

July 11, Sunday, 1943

Got up at 7:00. Went on duty washing beds etc. Went to church, had the rabbi. Then unpacked the mattresses & carried them. The air corps were over for church & even they helped everyone in & out. We worked hard all day setting things up & doing the floor work with Crowley & Benzon. Washed my hair, wrote Bob a letter. Washed clothes & then took a shower after supper in the new mess hall. Heeny read her diary & we wrote letters.

July 12, Monday, 1943

Started out early on the Ward fixing it up, had mosquito netting & all, it looks swell now. Everyone was in & out. It was very hot after dinner & we sat around writing letters etc. & Maj. Silma & Maj. Penner told us the funny incidents of them stealing our food & water. Washed down on Ward. I fixed my tent a bit & then wrote letters again.

July 13, Tuesday, 1943

Went on duty at 7:00 am. Wrote letters etc. A lot of people were in visiting Sgt. Dowd etc. It was very, very hot & we rested all afternoon. Mary was going to try & get Bob in Don's outfit & he said it wouldn't do any good because he was going to be transferred up here soon anyhow. Emptied my bag & fixed up again.

July 14, Wednesday, 1943

Have a cold. Got in more supplies today but didn't work hard. General Blese was here today & ate in our mess hall. I'm beginning to like the outfit better. Maj. Silner is swell & Capt. Dock & Sgt. Dowd are all fun. Maj. Silner had us all up in Ward for champagne. Fixed up my tent again & then went to the wreck hall.

July 15, Thursday, 1943

Still no patients. We're all getting to know one another much better and I think we're going to be happier. We're still restricted. Got a lot of mail, had none from Bob. Took a shower, washed my hair & got some work done in the tent. They put up a sign outside our tents because we're living like Arabs.

July 16, Friday, 1943

It's a thrill to watch the planes go off & then come back in such a beautiful way. Our first patients come, casualties from Sicily were the first in the invasion. Still no letter from Bob.

July 17, Saturday, 1943

Messed around all morning on the Ward. In the afternoon I took 2 hours off, did washing etc. Then they blew the bridge again and several more patients came in. We get 16 malaria patients. Staery fixed us wooden boxes for dressers. Had 2 letters from home. In the evening we were out of restriction.

July 18, Sunday, 1943

Had fun on the Ward. Went to church & it was packed. Couldn't get another person in. Had officers & air corps Chaplain from across the street. Received a letter from Bob which he said he had written the night he got back. It was sweet & I have a feeling he's coming in the evening, there were dates galore & this lawyer from AM & Cincy came after me but I didn't know it was for tonight.

July 19, Monday, 1943

We were busy on the Ward, admitted 12 more malaria & the bugle was flowing all day for the letter hearers. It was very very hot today. In the evening at 7:15 we had memorial services for Allen. It was very touching & there was quite a crowd. The first & I hope the only one. Lt. Cohen from the air corps is the one who was here last night. Stayed in tonight.

July 20, Tuesday, 1943

Day of days. We meet again. I was going into the mess hall & heard someone totting. I looked around & there he was. I could have fainted. No lunch & rode in Jeep up to Ward & to see Brownie & Lt. Muller was more arrogant for him to see the Cal. His convoy arrived at 12:15 & he was here at 12:30. We went for a ride in nature and what a reunion. The Colonel was very nice to him. He met Maj. Silner & everyone was so glad to see him. He's miles away but couldn't come back today.

July 21, Wednesday, 1943

Went down to extension area to work. Saw first very real war casualties, burns, bullet wounds etc. Helped Capt. Walters do dressings, then evacuated some. Made up more beds with mattresses. He was in the ward & down at the camp but I didn't get to see him. He brought me a beautiful nurse's watch & then came in the evening & we went for a ride & watched the places in the sunset. He has really changed & is sweeter than ever. We came back & there was a blackout & had to go on the Ward after working hard all day. Patients galore. The mess boys brought our patients sandwiches and coffee.

July 22, Thursday, 1943

Worked down at the Extension area again & worked like dogs. He was down there to see me but I was resting & they left me sleep. In the evening he came back again & we went down in the Wd. for a drink & were talking to everybody & then went to the movie on the hill "Cowboy in Manhattan." I came back & got chairs. We were fairly comfortable. I love him better every day.

July 23, Friday, 1943

Worked 7-12:30 in the cont. camp making cots. Bob came over & we talked & he helped me make up cots. In the afternoon, he & Hebel came after me & we went to Bizerte in Mediterranean, went swimming. We had a wonderful time & felt so close, the three of us. Shined dog tags in the sand. I was all dry & ready to put on my slacks & was helping them struggle with shoes & socks. Wd. & he told me he practically worshipped me & that he'd rather kiss me than do anything in the world, even eat. He was going to teach me to drink & he also told me he was jealous on the beach & wished we were married. Then I missed Hebel with socks & the two of them threw me back in the Med. Sea. I lost a shoe & he found it & they got all wet again & so was I. We are going to be married as soon as possible. His driver brought us gobs of grapes. He brought me home & came back early & we went for a ride & sat & planned & it started to rain.

July 24, Saturday, 1943 - AFRICA

This date will hover over me forever. Bob was coming to see Lt. Stock & myself & I waited and waited then went to Miss Chamberlain's office. She told me. I met Lt. Ballard in a daze then Capt. Price & Lt. Miller piled me in a car & brought me up. All the kids & Miss Chamberlain were good but I almost went crazy until Lt. Hebel & Clark came after me & took me down to the camp & I saw the Major & he said I was to be one of them & treated me wonderful because he was so sorry for everything then Hebel & Clark took me and waited on me hand & foot. We went to the refuge & he had asked for him & then went to air corp mess & then the long ride back was so comforting. Clark got dead drunk on purpose then all of us stopped and sobbed until we got it out of us. Then the driver took Clark home & Hebel sat on a hill in our area for an hour and a half & we talked & he told me everything.

July 25, Sunday, 1943

Didn't feel like ever waking up. Couldn't look at the sun it was so beautiful. Folded gauze in Miss Cham. room & all the kids were in & I thought I just couldn't stand it. Then they took me to church & I felt better when I got back. Miss Cham. said Hebel was to see me & he told me of the funeral arrangement. He picked me up at 2:00 and Browne, Crowley & Lt. Miller followed. Procession and tribute was at 4:00. 8 trucks, 7 Jeeps & a command car. It was beautiful with white crosses, creeks, trees and mountains. The boys visited & Hebel took me & the rest were in back of us. They had an organ, violin and singer. "Beautiful Life of Somewhere" and "Till We Meet Again". The sermon & the salute while they play Taps, the first time we'd heard it since we pledged to remember. They took me back to their comp & gave me some treasure & a picture. I wore my Signal Corp pin on the outside over my heart.

July 26, Monday, 1943

Slept down in HD quarters with Porta, her father died. I overslept & got coffee late & then went up on Bernards Ward with Capt. Eddie Weinstein. I thought I was going crazy & couldn't stand it. I worked hard & wrote home & felt some better in the afternoon. After I got off duty Lt. Miller called me & there stood Clark & Hebel grinning all over, I really adopted them. They were going for coffee & doughnuts but first we went to see Biggy in the Jeep. I walked to the Jeep with them & Hebel gave me the champagne ribbons & we planned to go tomorrow night to get away again. Then I went to see Biggie after taking a shower.

July 27, Tuesday, 1943

Enjoyed work on the Ward somewhat more which helped to ease the pain. Washed in my hours off. Brownie brought me my mail then at 7:00pm after trying to see how I felt asked if I could stand a letter from Bob & oh how happy it made me. It was so beautiful at times when I let myself think of it and I get alone I almost go panicky and feel I can't stand it, but then someone always comes along and I can go on. Everyone is simply marvelous to me. Clark & Hebel came over & took Biggy & I for a ride to some bakery comp & I bought a Valetta cheese I had from home. They made it a pleasant evening & then asked to go to Carthage & got a PM Friday. I know Bob would be glad because they're nice to me because otherwise I think I'd go crazy.

July 28, Wednesday, 1943

It was a little better today but it is still so very horrible to believe all our plans smashed. Wrote a letter to his mother & one home. The Ward really takes any mind off myself. Lt. Ballard came up & talked to me for a long time & everyone is so nice. Hebel & Clark didn't come last night but we had a movie "Mr. Deeds Goes to Town," so that helped.

July 29, Thursday, 1943

Had another 10-12 off & have very nice patients. Really enjoyed working with them. Stayed home in evening. Clark was up & said they'd be over for us early. Lupe came over & talked to me & so did Bissonette & felt very blue again. Wrote letters. Received 12.

July 30, Friday, 1943

Worked 7-12:30. Enjoyed duty this AM. Some very nice, understanding boys. Received 9 more letters. Hebel & Clark picked us up about 2 & they have to sign in & out, even for us. We had a nice ride to Carthage with the roof down. Had a guide take us through cathedral museum. Then went back to Tunisia & the boys went in to the refuge & bought wine to take back & we remembered last Saturday. Then we rode about halfway home to a river & sat on the sand & had a picnic. It was a beautiful evening. Then we went for a ride & picked up 2 Lts and took them home & they told us about a nice place to go in Ferryville. The boys have really been sweet to me & I had a nice time.

July 31, Saturday, 1943

The boys on our Ward are swell. Took shower, washed my hair & washed my clothes. Got a lot more mail. Had a steak supper @ 7:30 at dedication of our Officer's Club. Then went over but didn't stay. As Cromley, Beazon & myself were walking up we met 2 nice Lts & we talked for a long time & then they watched a movie with us. It was the movie I'd seen with him at Camp DeShone. I was feeling terribly, terribly blue because it had just been a week ago. Couldn't stand it and had to leave.

MEMORANDA

Dear diary: This has been the most tragic & also most beautiful month I'll ever put in. I hurt & ache all over when I think of it but I know I'll have to stand it. God only knows how much we loved one another and it doesn't seem at all fair but he must have had a reason. I can't believe it yet he was so adorable & real & alive.

August 1, Sunday, 1943

Went to church. The air corps really has a beautiful service. Had a 1-3 off. Nothing unusual happened. Rather a dull day. Spent the evening talking with different kids & they all told me how wonderful he was.

August 2, Monday, 1943

Was fairly busy today. Helped Eddie do 2 spinals. Hebel was up in the afternoon & asked me to go out last night. He & Clark came about 7:30 but we didn't leave until 8 because Biggie was busy. We rode to Bizerte & went swimming. The sound of the waves was very nice. They brought a radio & wine & we had chuckles. Had a nice time but coming back we got lost and we were ½ hour late. I hope Hebel doesn't start getting funny now. Gibbons was telling me Lt. Cohen is crazy about me & that they know about Bob and don't even know Cohen. We had to walk up the hill at 12:30am.

August 3, Tuesday, 1943

Had a grand time on the Ward. Intended to stay home in the evening & read & write letters. Capt. Price fixed our late slip up so we didn't get called. Then the kids dragged me & dressed me & at about 10:00pm went over to air corps party with Lt. Harrigan & nephew of Harrigan, went with Lt. Doris & DeWitt. They were all swell & we had cake & everything. Bob Harrigan was very sweet & understood because his fiancé had been killed. We went for gas & he asked me for a date for Thursday. Pleasant evening.

August 4, Wednesday, 1943

Had a 1-3 off. Got more sun tan. Hebel came up on the Ward & stayed & talked for about 2 hours. He is really swell. Brought me a comb & said he'd try & get back for the movie but they were going on a job pretty far from here. I told him should price fixing us up. In evening sent Harrigan a note so he'd come Friday so I could go tomorrow. Went to movie "Pride of the Yankees" but didn't ever wait for it to start, we were so sleepy & the air corps argued with us to stay, but we didn't.

August 5, Thursday, 1943

Had a PM and got a lot done & got some more sun tan. Went to E.B.S. party on truck with a gang of swell kids but had a miserable time. All old drunken Cols. & Maj. & they danced & sang & I couldn't stand it. I wanted to scream. I wanted Bob so badly. Some of them 4th enoc nurses brought me back & I went up on the WD with Marge & Lutz and they made me feel better. Then some of our boys came over & kidded & then walked me home. I cried for about an hour and felt better.

August 6, Friday, 1943

Had a 10-12 off & got pretty much done. Came off duty just hoping Lt. Harrigan couldn't come. Felt blue & longed for Bob. Wrote letters. They came & Klein & another Lt. went & they took us over to the plane. Fastened me in parachute & all the other chains, put on the helmet goggles, microphone & earphones & closed me in. Showed me all the gun switches & bombs light & everything. Let me shift the rudder in the back. It was really a thrill. Then we went for a ride and picked grapes out of the orchard, and went to the club and got a drink & went to their tent & talked with several other fellows. It was a pleasant evening.

August 7, Saturday, 1943

Was awakened at 4:00am by sound of bombing, awakened all the kids & we watched Pardon Brite Harbor until 5:00am. Looked like the 4th of July. Bullets, flares, planes & spotlights. German planes flew overhead. It was the closest raid since they bombed Mateur. Had a PM & Col. Donnelly & all inspected & said our Wd. looked nice. Lt. Phillips told me all about Bob & what they did & how much he loved me for about an hour. Didn't do anything but went to the movie & then they asked for volunteers to help with a hundred new patients so we went down. They were casualties from Sicily & were such darling patients & so appreciative. They got fixed up, then fed. Sgt. Dowd & Sgt. Sandy & all were there.

August 8, Sunday, 1943

Went to church – nice sermon. Then had 10-12 off. Bernard has a PM. Received a letter from home all about Bob. I couldn't help but cry. At suppertime I went in Miss Chamberlain's office with the report & she was talking to a Lt. then she came running after me & asked me to go with him. I told her I couldn't & then she called in the mess hall. I couldn't refuse so I met him in the N.O. Lt. Russ Bakery, cute looking & cocky & reminded me so much of Bob. His ideas about things & he even rode down to 30th signal to turn around then we rode to Pigert to eat but were too late so sat on the beach. The last place Bob and I went together & when he started getting affectionate I had to cry.

August 9, Monday, 1943

Didn't do anything unusual. Had a PM. Was going with June but didn't. Stayed in & washed my hair & wrote letters etc. Went to bed early. Jean & Miss Chamberlain went with Bakery & Capt. Geo.

August 10, Tuesday, 1943

Worked pretty hard all day & then worked on 7-10. Lt. Harrigan & another Lt. came over & wanted me to go out so I told Harrigan he could come Wed. We were busy & horrible losses. Thurmond was killed in a Jeep accident. Henry and Hesse were hurt. Can't understand what's going on.

August 11, Wednesday, 1943

Nothing unusual happened on duty. Was expecting Russ Bakery to go to Sicily but when I came back from supper there he sat with a friend of his. So I had to write Harrigan a note. We went to Bizerte & had a steak supper & had pretty much fun. But he drinks too much. He wants me to go steady & I don't want to but I told him he could come back Friday & he wanted to take me to Tunis.

August 12, Thursday, 1943

Worked all day. Nothing unusual happened. Cleaned my tent up & fixed it all up. Still miss Bob terribly sometimes. Can't get him off my mind.

August 13, Friday, 1943

We were supposed to move down to the tent but they kept putting it off so that we didn't get any time to go to supper with Lt. Bakery at 5:00 but he sent a note that he couldn't come & I was glad because I was tired but then Lt. Harrigan came & I had to go down & sit & talk to him. Gave him some books for his roommate.

August 14, Saturday, 1943

Moved down to tent city. Have 4 end Wards. Had fun fixing them up but got no time off at all & was dead tired. In evening Lt. Harrigan was coming over for the movie but it was cancelled so he & Lt. Huntington & Anderson & I went to their club & they all came around and told riddles. Then he drove over & got a book for me. It was a beautiful moonlight night.

August 15, Sunday, 1943

Down in the tents, like it now. Starting to get arranged, have good kids working with me. Come up to church on shuttle bus & walked down with Sgt. Moody. Was off 3-5 & visited Hesse. When trying to get transportation Lt. Stock came up & asked me to get a PM Thursday & asked if I would be scared to take a ride over to Sicily in a B25. I jumped at the chance. Had fun with patients. Stayed home.

August 16, Monday, 1943

Really getting a good set-up now & have fun. New nurses in to help. All
the fellows are still trying to talk me into giving them my place. We had a
fire in the pts. mec hall tent. The eng. came over & took us too & we had
a delicious supper with ice cream & then played games. Came home so
blue with no reason & cried for 2 hours. I miss him so.

August 17, Tuesday, 1943

Had a PM but didn't get to go with Lt. Stock. Stayed in & washed &
slept. In evening went to see Bob Hope & Francis Langford in person
in EX unit. Went down with Lt. Lesnick & Eddie Weinstein. Had fun &
got picked up with Col. Carolitz gang. Then went to visit Heronn & we
had another air raid in Bizerte & Ferryville.

August 18, Wednesday, 1943

Nothing unusual happened. Good time on duty with Sgts. They're cute.
In evening went to see "Golden Boy" with Bissionette & my patients
sat with us. Ruben & I were so sad I had to cry practically all the way
through & then had to get up and leave & cried for about an hour & then
Alma and Biss. calmed me down. I was nervous. We had another big air
raid.

August 19, Thursday, 1943

Was very busy & hot & terribly blue for Bob. Patients & all made me
nervous. Came off & Leona asked me to go with her & air corp to their
club. Had a nice time & they were fun. Steered the Jeep all the way
home. Made me miss Bob more than ever.

August 20, Friday, 1943

Had fun on duty today. The patients are all cute. I talked about Bob for
about 2 hours. Simon told me Russ was looking all over for me. DeWitt
asked me to go with her and her English friend. Rode to Ferryville in
a beautiful Mercury coupe & then met Capt. Cliff Baker of air corp.
Darling & helped on planes on raid over Sicily. Had fun finding the
dance & then met Lemley there from 80th. Had to leave because of
suspected air raid.

August 21, Saturday, 1943

Had a nice time on duty, the boys are all cute. In evening went to movie and saw "Stage Door Canteen." Received a letter from home & they know now. The movie got me again as usual. It was sort of sad.

August 22, Sunday, 1943

Went to church. It was nice but made me choke up as usual. I like to work with Capt. Duch & have swell kids. Honey Simon & O'Brien on our Wd. We're always planning our party in Cincy. Sgt. Sheir & all. Stayed home & slept instead of going to movie.

August 23, Monday, 1943

Enjoyed duty as usual. Got my watch from him back with the crystal on it. Fellow hitched a ride from Sicily. Received a letter from Hebel today. He's very sweet and I imagine will be back soon. "I'm stepping out with a memory tonight."

August 24, Tuesday, 1943

Really enjoy working in tent city now. Was CQ 7-10 & had a nice time entertaining all the dates but it really made me long for Bob all the more. I'll never get over missing him.

August 25, Wednesday, 1943

Had 3 pts. go over the hill and come back very drunk. Had fun transferring them up to 17. In evening took my laundry over & shoes to get fixed & had fun talking to the fellows in front of visit supply. Swell kids. If only Bob were here. Slept through another air raid.

August 26, Thursday, 1943

Had a PM. Stayed in washed my hair & washed clothes. Went to see Henry. After supper went to see the "Awful Truth" with Cary Grant. He reminds me so much of Bob. He is darling, crazy & cocky.

August 27, Friday, 1943

NO ENTRY.

August 28, Saturday, 1943

Worked all day in tent city. Had the blues so went to 38th service party
& hotel. Wore beige suit & very first dance Lt. Neumann attached
himself to me. Excellent orchestra, good food. Good dancer. Wanted to
take me home & wanted a date. He was nice and funny. They played us
"As Time Goes By" & "Sleepy Time Gal" then Jeep crashed. I thought
I was going to be killed. Neumann was sweet. X-ray & anesthesia after
receiving WD. 16. – 3AM.

My grandmother had a severe arm injury and was writing with opposite hand.

August 29, Sunday, 1943

Groggy & miserable all day. Had a lot of visitors but I couldn't talk to
them. Vomited all over. Took me to x-ray.

August 30, Monday, 1943

Much more comfortable but still in pretty much pain. Everyone was in
again. Lt. Clark was in this afternoon. Col. Lande & whole bunch were
in. Lt. Neumann spent the evening.

August 31, Tuesday, 1943

A lot more visitors. Everyone was in. Got a bouquet of flowers from my
patients.

September 1, Wednesday, 1943

Party at the officers club.

September 2, Thursday, 1943

Hebel came back and we went to the movie.

September 3, Friday, 1943

Italy invaded.

September 4, Saturday, 1943

People in & out.

September 5, Sunday, 1943

Heaney & Jean packed, Mary fixed me for party. Clark & Hebel took me to 300th sig officer movie. Paratrooper bombed. Harrigan was here & so was Neumann. Movie. Party in officers mess.

September 6, Monday, 1943

Kids & out. Neumann was here. Went to see Hammond. Sgt. Shiler & Sgt. Steck were here. Watched a raid. Saw plane go. Ack, ack.

September 7, Tuesday, 1943

Left 3rd General in Matteau.

Good luck Arlene.
I will see you for that trip.
Mary

So long tent neighbor. See you soon – Love always.
McBrowning.

September 8, Wednesday, 1943

Typed letters in Scotty's office. Nothing unusual. Passed Algeria.

September 9, Thursday, 1943

General alum @ 10PM – 3:18AM. 2:30AM this afternoon – Italians on deck singing thorough. After dinner Italians left ship in harbor at Oran.

September 10, Friday, 1943

Stayed in Oran Harbor until 5PM after getting oil. Visited Lt. patients on deck & after supper had fun out on deck with Coleman & gang.

September 11, Saturday, 1943

Spent the morning in the Strait of Gibraltar, the Rock & Spain. Typed letters in the afternoon.

September 12, Sunday, 1943

Everyone is sea sick. Spent a lot of time with Coleman & he gave me his picture.

September 13, Monday, 1943

Most of them not feeling well. Was going to help Scotty but didn't get around to it. Capt. Phalkino convinced me I should take the ring off & put it on my dog tags.

September 14, Tuesday, 1943

Everyone better & cheerful. Beautiful full moon.

September 15, Wednesday, 1943

Load time. Went to patients birthday party.

September 16, Thursday, 1943

Read. Had fun with Maj. Small & Col. Nenn trying to, Coleman & myself watched flying fish & phas. Had fun & got Mr. Casey's insignia. The eternal triangle removed Bob's insignia.

September 17, Friday, 1943

Mr. Goldman took Ann & Coleman & I on the Bridge. Shot the sun with Sextant. Had a funeral at sundown for a sailor overboard.

September 18, Saturday, 1943

Took sun bath – both with suit on. Had a lot of fun out on deck. Such a crazy bunch. Coleman gave me his insignia. Had alert again in the afternoon.

September 19, Sunday, 1943

Bad night. Very windy and dropped depth charges etc. Very rough all day. Sat on the deck all day.

September 20, Monday, 1943

One of the nurses washed my hair. We dressed for dinner & had our pictures taken. Sat outside & talked. More depth changes.

September 21, Tuesday, 1943

Master at arms gave me the flag. We were escorted in Pained, Coleman was excited but I had a funny feeling seeing the statue for Bob & resolved to go back & come in the right way. We sat on the deck & AFM brought me back a CMM.

Mt. Sinai, New York

September 22, Wednesday, 1943

Had breakfast & lunch on ship, had doughnuts and milk. Had fun with 3rd mate & everyone saying goodbye. Had band and "As Tme Goes By". Came to receiving officers in & went on WD21. In evening went to stage show with Coleman after calling home.

September 23, Thursday, 1943

Tried to get money and baggage. Borrowed money from Coleman & got permanent from Cadre & then RK fellows all over. I went to see Ann.

September 24, Friday, 1943

Got into baggage & had France changed. Went to PX for Ann. In evening rode to Staten Island with RC. Then some people, Peggy and Leo, Rich showed us N.Y. and Radio City, etc. Civilian rode us home with a cute Lt. on crutches.

September 25, Saturday, 1943

Cool. Read in afternoon. Sgt. Schulze brought all his family & wife to see me. Went to PX & movie. After supper Mrs. Sullivan gave me a copy of her poem.

September 26, Sunday, 1943

Slept late. Went to church. Went to baggage room and to see Ann. Called home & read. In evening went to nurses quarters with Goldstein & saw everyone at the PX & she wanted to hear the story about Bob.

September 27, Monday, 1943

Got orders that we were leaving at 1:00PM, the boys came over and said goodbye. Spent the afternoon with Coleman then heard we weren't leaving until tomorrow. He bought me a malted & we went to the cleaners. Read in evening.

September 28, Tuesday, 1943

Messed around all morning. After lunch Coleman came after me & I walked over with him to get his coat & then Capt. Baumgartner went with us to PX & we had Cokes. Coleman bought me almonds & I waited until his bus came to take him to Yale & we said goodbye. We left about 4:30 & the train pulled out about 5. – Compartment.

September 29, Wednesday, 1943

Arrived at Ashford at 9:30. Gorgeous place. Stolze is our day nurse & Stanley our NN. Met Ratliff all other kids from 25th. They took us all over the place & to casino for supper. Then went to Broadcast & to PX.

September 30, Thursday, 1943

Nothing unusual happened. Wrote letters, talked with boys, officers & enlisted men. Went to movie at PX.

MEMORANDA

Unhappy, uncomfortable, unsettled, restless.

October 1, Friday, 1943

Saw Maj. Keller. Had x-ray. Went to library & read.

October 2, Saturday, 1943

Sat & read, listened to organ. Miss Bob so much it hurts. Called home & I have a letter from Hebel & 2 others rode with Stan & kids to town & saw "Hostage" in evening & then PX.

October 3, Sunday, 1943

Slept late & after lunch went for a ride to Eagles Nest & had chicken with kids. Came back & saw "Destroyer."

October 4, Monday, 1943

Had cast taken off this afternoon, it's wonderful. They want me to go on a Bond tour. Had chat in lobby with Kirk's friends, Huttle & gang. Went with Jeanette to see "So Proudly We Hail."

October 5, Tuesday, 1943

Sat around & read. Went to movie in evening & had trouble with drunk in PX.

October 6, Wednesday, 1943

Got paid & visited with Marty Cosner. Called home again & have another letter from Hebel.

October 7, Thursday, 1943

More mail, none important. Went to matinee "Best Foot Forward". Darling. Had drain removed, no leave 6 weeks to beauty parlor. Casino for supper with kids to movies again then to casino with Staley and several Lts. Had a nice time. Took Kirk to station for leave.

October 8, Friday, 1943

Received my mail. Hebel is sweet. Sat in lobby with kids. Alex & I walked into town. Stolze had me try on a formal & they fixed me up with a date with an MAC who brought his friend up to my room to find out about Walts. I didn't want to go but I guess I'll have to. Wrote letters after going to PX. Sweet kid Peck in x-ray.

October 9, Saturday, 1943

Nothing unusual during the day. At 8 o'clock I went with Dan, MAC & Stan with Moe (neuro surgeon). Had darling red sling with butterfly which made a hit with everyone. Had gobs of fun at the steak supper forming our emer. unit & they all tease & razz me all the time. Danced & danced. Moe introduced me to all his big shots as his future wife & asked me to go to movie with him tomorrow night. Waited for the dress then brought her up on the Ward & drank milk in the kitchen & Stolze worked for her.

Moe and Arlene.

October 10, Sunday, 1943

Slept late. Went to have dressings changed & sat out on veranda with Moe, Don, Aleck & gang and had fun. Went to christening with Alex & in evening he kept calling & looking for me & I was in one of the cottages. He met me in lobby for movie after. I bought a ticket & he showed me pictures of his family & then we walked to the casino. He's very sweet, kind & considerate. We poured out our hearts' story to each other.

October 11, Monday, 1943

Had drain changed & Lt. Reith said I could have a Leave. Sat in lobby with gang & Moe & Jack & they were planning the wedding. Met him at 9:00 & we went down to casino & discussed life & faith in general & he told me how much everyone & he liked me. We went for a walk to the lake & he was like a little boy holding my hand & asking to kiss me & go with him. He put me on train & is swell. Rode train.

October 12, Tuesday, 1943

Slept late. Then A&D groups to orientation meeting in lounge. Running around with Wadsmith. Wrote letters & played cards & met several nice officers but not any comparison to last year. Mail from home, Hebel & Moe.

October 13, Wednesday, 1943

2 carriages & presents. Went to Aunt Erna's for supper with gang.

October 14, Thursday, 1943

Family saw me off at the station. Nice train. Met Moe & Sgt. Schaffer at Charleston. Had fun between his becoming an American & me becoming his fiancé. The boys just ribbed him to death and made him treat practically the whole train for dinner. Jack met us at the station & thought we were married because of my flowers. We saw ½ the movie then he visited in my room with Alex & I & then we went to the casino & he brought me home the long way.

October 15, Friday, 1943

Wrote letters etc. Showed Maj. Antapal 3rd General pictures. Sat in lobby with gang. Went to casino with Moe – had fun with Don, Bob, Jack, Don & Capt. Abrams etc. It rained again. He says he really likes me. I guess he does.

October 16, Saturday, 1943

Rained. Moe was up all morning & we sat in wreck room. Capt. Harris' wife came in from train accident. Moe ate lunch with us. Then we sat around & he & I went for a walk & I felt blue because I couldn't go back with him. Then the dedication we had to stand retreat & to the Peek's for cocktails then to restaurant for steak & to movie then casino & to the chicken shack with Capt. Abrams & Fran. Good long day.

October 17, Sunday, 1943

Sleepy all morning. Moe called me at 2:00 & we all met the Peek's in the lounge then we went to tea for Col. Carter & came back & we walked them down town & said goodbye. Then I treated him on his citizenship to steak at the casino. Then we went to Don McCurry's cottage & to movie. Then Sonny brought Southern Comfort at farewell to Aleck's. We almost had a fight. Took them to the station then walked home & sat on veranda & talked for a long time. I had the blues.

October 18, Monday, 1943

Had fun all day. Went to USO show with Moe, Don & Sonny. It was lousy. Then they all met me in the lobby & Jack gave me a chrysanthemum & he, McDool & I drilled all the way down to the casino. Had fun.

October 19, Tuesday, 1943

Had both meals together & sat with gang in lobby & then had a talk with Sonny after he & Moe finished a game of ping pong & Moe went to study. Wish I didn't like him so much. We all 3 went to the movies & then we went to the casino & sat on the porch afterWard.

October 20, Wednesday, 1943

Had cold. In bed late & Moe came in & wakened me & came & got me at noon. Gave me his papers to read & then we went for a wonderful walk on golf course to lake. Had supper with Capt. Abrams & then met Sonny & they played basketball & I watched. Stopped in for a Coke & then met train but Alex missed it. Came up to my room and had brown cows. Then Sonny left us alone. I wish he could get straightened out.

October 21, Thursday, 1943

Had fun all day with DelHarris & Marty. After supper Moe & I went to town & bought Jack's wedding present. Then we went to movie with Jack & saw "Thank Your Lucky Stars". Then to casino after which we sat in swing & on front porch for a while.

October 22, Friday, 1943

Del awakened me early & we went down & took pictures of Capt. Abrams, then we went to PX after which I went to the beauty parlor. Had dinner with Moe & then sat in organ room. Went to Aleck's room & listened to the radio & wrote letters. He was called out constantly. – Moe O.D.

October 23, Saturday, 1943

Met Moe at noon then he came up to my room & slept. Then went to Jack's wedding. Took pictures of Maj. Woodhall & family. Met the Harrises & Bob. Went down to casino for steak supper. Then to movie & then downtown for pie & coffee. After which we went to Don's cottage, almost broke up.

October 24, Sunday, 1943

Awakened Moe at 11:15 & met him in the lounge & had lunch & then we all sat in the organ room & listened to the concert & then had teas while gang of us took pictures. Then we all went to the casino & had fun. After supper we wrote letters until we went to see "Sahara" then to casino again & had sandwiches in kitchen.

October 25, Monday, 1943

Had usual time in lobby, had lunch & dinner with Moe. Approx. 6 of us
pts. came in, 7 nurses. After supper we met Sonny & we went to their
basketball practice & then to drug store. Jack & Don & RC Walters &
myself watched. Then we sat on the porch & talked.

October 26, Tuesday, 1943

Worked 7-5:15 on Ward in nursery. Had lunch & dinner with Moe.
Then went to movie, then went to casino.

October 27, Wednesday, 1943

Worked 8-12 with Ruby. Slept in afternoon. Moe received telegram from
Vicki, he was so excited. Had supper together then listened to music &
went to Jack's & wrote letters & waited for Vicki's call. She loves him &
wants to marry him when she comes back. He still says he's marrying me
in a second if it weren't for her. Then we went down to the club.

October 28, Thursday, 1943

Worked. Had lunch & dinner with Moe & went to movie and saw
"Sweet Rosie O'Grady" then went down to casino & had sandwiches.
We all stood around and had a good time. P.S. Capt. Harris drove us to
town but stores were closed.

October 29, Friday, 1943

Worked in morning & again from 6-10. Moe was up. Went to casino &
sang again. Had good time.

October 30, Saturday, 1943

After lunch with Capt. Harris & Moe as per usual we went to the
laundry & back up to get Capt. Harris & sat in lobby. Then went to
Lewisburg & picked up soldiers along the way. He bought Vicki & Mary
a present & then I bought shirts etc. It was a nice ride. Got the pictures
from the drug store. After supper I wrote letters & then wore my new
blouse & we went to the Halloween party with Jack & Guermon. Jack
was drunk. Then met Rabeze who came down for weekend. Had fun
after the orchestra.

October 31, Sunday, 1943

Called him at 11:15. Met him for lunch. Sat in sun then went to play on bundling then went to visit Jack & Pat & took pictures. Then back to supper. While he studied I went to see Rabeze & kids then we went to movie then to casino. I had the blues & he brought me in then called him & apologized.

MEMORANDA

Feel much better. My arm is better & also my spirits. Moe helped a lot & we've had a lot of fun. It's wonderful knowing a person like him.

November 1, Monday, 1943

Had supper then listened to music. Wrote letters. Moe worked in evening & then we went downtown & got me food.

November 2, Tuesday, 1943

Received a bunch of letters. Sat in lobby & then Moe came up & we sat in Wd. living room & wrote letters & I bought cakes & we listened to the radio. Rained all night. Went for a walk in it.

November 3, Wednesday, 1943

Received 2 letters, another one from Hebel. Had lunch & supper with Moe. Made a crazy bet with him for after the war. Then went down to casino. Moe didn't feel well at all.

November 4, Thursday, 1943

After lunch we borrowed Clane's car & Moe changed his clothes then we took them down to the cleaners & tried to get the pictures. It was a beautiful day. Kirk was given cottage – Kansas C. Helped her move. She had supper with us. Then we showed Moe the place & he & I had argument over going over there, but he met me for the movie. Jack & Pat went. Then we went to casino & he brought me right home & didn't even kiss me. I'm getting the jitters. Can't stand to argue.

November 5, Friday, 1943

Had usual mealtime. Rendezvous then after supper got our things together & went over to Kirk's living room. Had fun writing letters, listening to radio etc. They played "People Will Say We're in Love" several times. He can be so sweet.

November 6, Saturday, 1943

He met me at noon & we ate with Don. Then sat in lobby & met Del & Bob. We rode with them to Lewisburg & we messed around, Don, Bob & us in bowling alley. Saw Sonny on Greyhound bus, got sundaes. Then we got a cab & stopped for the pictures then walked back & went to Don's & helped Bob move in. We had fun, then all got cleaned up & went down to the casino & met the Harrises. Then Moe was called out for case, went back to the harp. Met Jack & Pat & went to show. It was good. Then went to casino.

November 7, Sunday, 1943

Another letter from Hebel. Met Moe for lunch. Gen. Marshall sat right across from us. Sat in lobby & listened to music with the Harris', Don, Terry & Bob. Then they went down to the casino while we came up after coat. We were all the way down & remembered we had forgotten it. Then back up again. Bought hot dogs & cakes & listened to the symphony in the Harrises. Waited in Moe's room while he got cleaned up, then we had supper. I met him again at 8:00 with Sonny & Jack & Pat. Saw "Flesh and Fantasy". Then we walked down town & got hamburgers.

November 8, Monday, 1943

Usual lunch & supper. Then he studied & I discovered U.S.O. show, better than usual. We went down to the PX for sandwiches, then used Kirk's living room, & ended up telling him about Bob & his funeral & I almost cried.

November 9, Tuesday, 1943

Usual lunch & dinner. After supper I wrote letters, then met him in the lobby & we went to see "Tornado.". The boys running the show wouldn't let me in until Moe told them I worked last week. Came up to my room & listened to the radio & wrote more letters & fell asleep. Then went to the kitchen and had milk.

November 10, Wednesday, 1943

Received a letter from Jeanie Cromly. Went downtown with Kirk & messed around looking for a present for Moe. Then came back & he met Rosemary & I & we went over Kirk's & had a fried chicken supper & listened to the radio.

November 11, Thursday, 1943

Moe came in early while I was still in bed & said they were going to stay 2 more months so we planned taking leaves. Waited for him & sat in back of show because pts. are not supposed to go to that one. Met Sonny, Jack & Pat. Then we went down Don & Bob's where Moe is going to live. Don & Bob both got drunk & Moe & I had a fight. Jack & Pat left early. We really have a problem for the next 2 months.

November 12, Friday, 1943

Now they tell me they can't give him a leave because he is a student. We messed around in the PX. etc. Had a late supper with Capt. Harris again. Then he came up to my room & took a nap while I wrote letters & then we went down to Jack & Pat's & had a very nice time in front of fire with their land lady reading our palms & Moe telling us about his hypnotism. Had cheese & crackers and wine.

November 13, Saturday, 1943

Had lunch & then came up to the room & I knitted as he read me the PM & then I taught him to knot & we went down to supper. Then I dressed & heard they were going formal so I got Jack to get my dress from the dry cleaners. Then we went to the basketball game. It was good but we lost. Barnes was kicked & Moe went out to take care of him then he helped button me up & I put his insignia on for him & we went to dance. Only music. Capt. Harris on piano. Nice time.

November 14, Sunday, 1943

Had chicken dinner in dining room with Moe, Don & Bob & then we read the funnies in the organ room, then to aud. & listened to mixed choir after which we walked downtown & then I wrote a letter & he studied as we waited for Don & Bob to pick us up & then we all went down to the casino for steak. Then he studied until we went to the movie & he came up to my room & left very coldly & I cried & got into pj's & he was back.

November 15, Monday, 1943

Had to go to PX for a sandwich cause he was late then Rosemary & Steve & I had to move together. After supper Don, Bob & I moved him over to Georgia & had fun.

November 16, Tuesday, 1943

Had about 5 min., left at noon to sit in lobby, stayed there with Moe. Had supper with them & then we went down to the PX with Sonny & met Jack & Pat and then we went over to the cottage & wrote letters but he spent most of the time reading his old letters.

November 17, Wednesday, 1943

Told Moe I guessed I had better just see him on a friendly basis etc. He was hurt. Got 25 letters in all yesterday & when he came at supper told me he got his orders & was getting his leave etc. After supper he was alternate O.D. & we went to the cottage & each planned our respective home & I gave him his birthday presents & combed both his & Bob's hair & then went down to the casino for a while & we had a fight & I came home & started up the elevator at 3 min. to 12:00 then ran back down & gave him a happy birthday kiss.

November 18, Thursday, 1943

He was busy in OR & all over so we didn't have much time at lunch or supper. Sonny came up at 6:00 & we were going to wait for him & go to the movie. He was in & out a half dozen times then couldn't go but worked up cases, so Sonny & I went & saw "True to Life" & came up & had sandwiches in the Wd. living room & after a while he had to go to work. He was so tired.

November 19, Friday, 1943

Had an operation which lasted till 2:30. Ate lunch with kids. He came after me at 2:30 & went to the PX while I tried to call home again about money but couldn't get them & then came in registered mail. Moe came early & we bought his ticket & went shopping for his family etc. Then he worked & I helped him mail out consultations etc. Then I helped him pack & get everything together & we went down to the casino. Then we made arrangements for the morning.

November 20, Saturday, 1943

Awakened at 3:30 when I heard a train & then N.M. awakened me at 5:15. Got dressed & took fruit over to Moe & helped him. He phoned for me at 5:30. Then we came over & signed out. It was foggy. Just had time for him to give me his address etc. Felt sort of lost. I walked back & stopped for coffee & then couldn't sleep till 8:30. Got up at 10 & took care of his PM newspaper & cashed checks etc. Went to matinee with kids & saw "Yankee Doodle Dandy." Very stirring. After supper listened to the organ, took a bath, wrote Moe & read. Miss him.

November 21, Sunday, 1943

Slept late. Went to church but couldn't get in. Had dinner with Kirk & Rosemary. People all asked me about Moe. Came up & read & wrote to Moe etc. Then had supper & listened to the organ & went to the movie. Sonny told me that people were talking & it made me very angry. Saw Olsen & Johnson came up & wrote to Neumann.

November 22, Monday, 1943

Went around and got all my stuff together. Packed & took some of my things over. Everyone knew I was going & about the orders & everything before I did. Walked to dry cleaners with Rosemary & listened to the organ. Received a card from Moe. Everyone said good bye.

November 23, Tuesday, 1943

The boys at the front deck kept teasing me about Moe & me going to meet him. No seats on train again. Sailor gave me his & I sat with Navy and Marine. Had fun. Family met me at train. Came right home. Picture of Bob is grand. Slept & then we went to go see Grandpa & Aunt Etta & took them to see Grace. Then saw Warren off at the station.

November 24, Wednesday, 1943

Messed around all day. Went to show and saw North Star. Met Port in lobby. Wrote to Moe after we came back.

November 25, Thursday, 1943

Went to football game. W.H. beat Elder 7-6. Had dinner at Aunt Erna's & took pictures with gang. Had supper after at Sgts. from air corp. Came with crazy kids & had a lot of fun dancing & everything. Got a telegram from Moe. Sent him one too.

November 26, Friday, 1943

Received 2 letters and a telegram from Moe & one from Hebel. Messed around all day. Went to Doloners in evening & they had a crowd. Stanley & Don & all went there including George's girlfriend.

November 27, Saturday, 1943

Another letter from Moe. Went to town & bought shoes & went to chiropodist & met Rosie & Bergmann. Came home & played piano & Glen & Donnie Gordon came over & we knitted.

November 28, Sunday, 1943

Went to church. Alma came home with me for dinner & we went over the river to Ft. Thomas to visit Storey's mother & sister & the Harrises.

November 29, Monday, 1943

Another letter from Moe. Met Sgts. Schultz & Marks at Union central and Lt. rode out to Lunken in staff car & then met Lt. Kottler & we worked on our interiors then went to the men's hall & then back up again & met the other boys. It wasn't bad & I wasn't so scared. He asked me questions & then we saw the movie afterWard, made plans for the boys to come out next Wed. & Lt. Kottler rode home with me in staff car & told me he'd only been here 10 days & felt alone etc. So he may come too. I got out in Cheviot and we met mom and dad.

November 30, Tuesday, 1943

Nothing unusual until Aunt Geneva called and was hostile & said she thought Grandpa Reuter was dead. When Daddy came we rushed down & he was sitting in the chair – shocking. Daddy and Gramma took it pretty well. All the relatives came down etc.

December 1, Wednesday, 1943

Stayed home. Nothing unusual. Daddy has a cold.

December 2, Thursday, 1943

Spent the day at Charlie Miller's funeral home. Crowds and crowds of people. Grandpa looked nice. Gobs of flowers.

December 3, Friday, 1943

Funeral at 10:30. Chas. drove our machine & went in first car. Went to Gramma's for lunch & I called Bar Bernard's family & Neumann's mother. Wrote cards for Aunt Geneva. Sympathy. Received calendar. Stayed home in evening.

December 4, Saturday, 1943

James & Mrs. Hahn came for supper & Arie came in evening & so did Weisses. Had nice time.

December 5, Sunday, 1943

Went to church in morning at Evang. Stayed home in afternoon. Aunt Geneva, Uncle Bill & Gramma were here for dinner & supper. Went to Schindlers in evening & all the gang was there including Bud & Bob.

December 6, Monday, 1943

Rained. Mom has cold. Received nice letter from Moe. Stayed home, messed around & baked cookies.

December 7, Tuesday, 1943

Helped mom wash & messed around all day.

December 8, Wednesday, 1943

Went to town. Met mom and Ruth May & we met everyone including Ferrels & Messmores. Ralph has his orders for morning. Another letter from Moe. After supper we took Carol & Betty & went to Angie's on Bracken & we entertained 5 air corps, Sgts. Had a nice time.

December 9, Thursday, 1943

Rode with Daddy & then got car & met Iney at Wigroom & we drove to Hamilton & had dinner with Jeanette & her mother in law. Jimmy is a doll. Iney & I had quite a talk about everything. They brought me home & I had a letter from Moe. Rosie called.

December 10, Friday, 1943

Went to town & met Pris. at her office. Then we went to the PO & I bought stamps, then to Caprone's after which we went to the Oldee "Bert Wheeler & Glen Miller singer" on stage & "Where Are My Children" on screen. Lot of soldiers in town.

December 11, Saturday, 1943

Went to town with mom & then we met Bert & we went to PO etc. & then to patio for turkey & then to see "Happy Land."

December 12, Sunday, 1943

Albert was in church. Surprise of surprises. Went to musical with Alma, Vera & her mother at the Sinton & then went for supper. The air corps Sgts. Called up & want me to come out.

December 13, Monday, 1943

Stayed home & messed around. Lots of mail, received 2 cards & 2 letters from Moe.

December 14, Tuesday, 1943

Stayed home & messed around. Received more from Moe. Listened to radio, etc.

December 15, Wednesday, 1943

Went to Gramma & Grandpa's for dinner & then to town & shopped around. Got lots of mail. 2 nice letters from Moe & then visited Aunt Pearl & Uncle Al & family and then Weiss.

December 16, Thursday, 1943

Ruth May stayed home in the morning. I went up to Good Sam in afternoon and visited & Daddy came up after meeting Gramma & her friends. More cards & 2 cards from Moe. Stayed home & listened to the radio & knitted.

December 17, Friday, 1943

Sgt. Sheldon called & said the dance on the 23rd is going to be at the Sinton. Stayed home & then met Ruth May, bought Moe's present.

December 18, Saturday, 1943

Met Pris. at noon in her office & then had lunch at Mullen's. Went to see "Arsenic and Old Lace," very good then shopped & had supper at Sidewalk Café in Gibson then to "His Butler's Sister" & then to Gramma's. 2 letters from Moe.

December 19, Sunday, 1943

To church & then to Bradfuerbers chicken dinner & then to Anna's & trimmed tree.

December 20, Monday, 1943

Stayed home & messed around.

December 21, Tuesday, 1943

Went to Northside Kirvoni's for lunch with Mom & Daddy then met Rena & visited all over. Went to town and put her on bus then messed around & met Alma, Vera & Beth & we went to Sidewalk Café. Received telegram about Dick being missing.

December 22, Wednesday, 1943

Long distance call from Moe & I tried sending another telegram to Maj. Kirkwood & Moe's going to try & fix things up. We went to Aunt Ida's for supper then came home & trimmed tree.

December 23, Thursday, 1943

Had to get ready. Ruth May stayed home & we messed around & then we had a very good supper after Dad & Don came down to see me, then we had our own Christmas Eve, just the family. Then went to Gramma and Grandpa's & down the station. Aunt Etta and Bert were there & Ruth May, Daddy, & Bert put me on the train. It was a nice train & came home with Lts. from Knox. We had fun.

December 24, Friday, 1943

Arrived at 6:45 & messed around & went to breakfast where I met Moe & Bob just coming in from trying to meet me at the station. They were all mixed up on the schedule. Then he came up & we talked & looked at Christmas cards etc. I was going to bed but everyone came in & Moe brought Bonnie in to meet me. She's cute. I slept then we had lunch & he had afternoon off & we went to Georgia D & then Bob went with us to supper & then we played around & then went down to see Dickens' "Christmas Carol" downtown. We all had the blues & I wanted to go in but they coaxed me to come back & we all had a long talk & I stayed till 1:30-2:00am. Bonnie called up to warn me about a pass.

December 25, Saturday, 1943

Went to dinner with Moe & sat with Del & Irv. Then sat in lobby & then went to Moe's office & talked & he told me if there was only Charlie he'd rather go with me. Went down to Jack & Pat's. Had egg nog & ice cream, coffee & champagne while they finished eating & then I helped Mrs. Kresnick with the dishes. Came back up for supper. It was very icy. Another card & Christmas package from Africa. Spent evening in. We almost broke up. Then they took turns reading. Ended up ok.

December 26, Sunday, 1943

Slept late & didn't eat waiting for Moe. They'd overslept till 11:45pm & then Bob phoned & met me. DeLucia phoned from Pitts. Moe, Bob & I went down to W.S.S. restaurant & met Jack & Pat. Had filet mignon for breakfast at 3:00pm. Then went for a walk & then went to Georgia D. Listened to the radio, read, knitted. Jack & Bob built a fire in the fireplace & the boys brought sandwiches & we sat around until we all went to the movie downtown & saw Gary Cooper. Bob phoned for me & I could stay out later.

December 27, Monday, 1943

Had lunch & supper with Moe. Received my mail. Messed around talking to kids etc. Sonny was up heckling for a while & then Moe came after working he & myself went down to the PX for cake & then I went to Georgia D. & we almost really had a battle, then we fixed it up but were so confused. Wants to go together but he can't control himself so we tried to figure & figure with still no solution. He even came up in our living room afterWards & we tried to talk it out.

December 28, Tuesday, 1943

Moe came dashing in at 10:30. Received orders to go to 35th at Attersburg on the 5th. He's going to get a leave. Had dinner & supper together. He's so excited & is OD. Stood on chairs & watched U.S.O. show. Went to his office & he gave me his picture. It made me feel funny. I went to the PX & got food. Moe & I had lunch in his office. He phoned home then after being called out several times, came in & visited for a while.

December 29, Wednesday, 1943

Had dinner with Moe but he was busy all afternoon & took Bonnie to supper. Then he came after me at 8:00. He fixed it up with Fred Cooper so I could have a pass till 1:00. We stopped in the PX for a cake then I packed for him while Bob & Moe heckled me. AfterWard he made love to me for the last time in thought & then he helped me get home with his junk & mine. Gully, he's so sweet & sincere & really likes me. It would be wonderful if he were in love with me, as far as I'm concerned, I'm all mixed up.

December 30, Thursday, 1943

Got up early & dashed to the station at 6:00. Met him & the train was going to be 2 hours late so we went back & had breakfast & then to Ga. D & he made love to me for the last time & probably forever & he was so sweet & wonderful. Came back & messed around all day & got frame for his picture & wrote letters. Bonnie & Sonny were up. Jack & Pat were up this afternoon.

December 31, Friday, 1943

Maj. Kirkwood came back & said as soon as my orders come through I could go to duty. Received 10 letters – good ones, Hebel, Koch, Gulmon etc. Went downtown & had my picture taken. Pat on formal in evening & messed around with patients. Then Jeanette came & I went AWOP to Marty & Jacks & we had nice quiet N.Y. & came home & wrote a long letter to Moe.

January 1, Saturday, 1944

Maj. Kirkwood said it wouldn't even be necessary to take another x-ray. Messed around then went to see "Coney Island," Betty Grable. After supper Jeanette called & I went over & visited.

January 2, Sunday, 1944

Slept late and missed church again. Went to dinner and then to matinee & saw "Government Girl" then in evening Don called me & went again to see it with Barb & Olive a RC worker. Then they arranged for a pass for me from Bob (OD) & we went to Olive's cottage & had milk, toast & coffee. The boys are so nice to me, I really appreciate it. It was rainy.

January 3, Monday, 1944

Nothing unusual happened. Got a lot of mail from Jimmy Coleman & Lt. Hackenworth & gobs of others. Read & wrote letters & finished Hebel's scarf.

January 4, Tuesday, 1944

Still haven't heard from Moe. Got pass & went down USS & got proofs & yarn. Nothing unusual happened. Read & wrote letters.

January 5, Wednesday, 1944

Received a card from Moe & several other interesting letters. Was talking to Irn & they said Don is leaving for Wash. DC for 2 months. Wrote letters etc.

January 6, Thursday, 1944

Went to breakfast with Moe & sat with Bob. Then went on duty in Central Supply & folded gauze. Received 2 cards from Moe. Still on his way. Gen. Eireholmes is here & made rounds. He's so sweet. Went to matinee "The Gang's All Here". Read & wrote letters.

January 7, Friday, 1944

C.S. & wore Burrows white uniform. Had more fun & did more things. Had supper with McDonnell, Rosemary & Bob then sat in Organ room with Bob & Jow & then Don came & Lt. Wrent & we had a lot of fun till 8:00 when Bob was going out. We came up & wrote letters.

January 8, Saturday, 1944

No entry.

January 9, Sunday, 1944

Went down W.S.S. restaurant with Bob for supper & then to movie with the kids.

January 10, Monday, 1944

No entry.

January 11, Tuesday, 1944

No entry.

January 12, Wednesday, 1944

No entry.

January 13, Thursday, 1944

No entry.

January 14, Friday, 1944

No entry.

January 15, Saturday, 1944

Worked split & went to movie then came up & wrote letters. Received just a card – really am getting tired of this place.

January 16, Sunday, 1944

Worked split & went to movie. Had fun with Bresler. Still getting good letters from Moe.

January 17, Monday, 1944

Worked straight & then went to the U.S.O show. Lot of good letters, one from Harrington. Went down to see Bresler with Rosemary, Neil & another kid.

January 18, Tuesday, 1944

Worked split. Maj. Woodhall told me I was leaving & we were going to see his pats. & Capt. Gulmon looked at the orders, no orders in N.O. – going to Billings where Moe was. Now I'm going to start my diary again. Went to movie & then called home long distance.

January 19, Wednesday, 1944

Slept late. Cleared the port & got record, said "Good Bye" to everyone & went down to Bob Bresler & Neal was lost on pursuing drink with them. Packed & messed around with the kids.

Indianapolis, Indiana

January 20, Thursday, 1944

Left on 3:45, had rest & comfy trip but was irritated with enlisted men. Met family at Cincy for ½ hour & arrived at Billings about 6:00. Had supper, met Cadaberg, Moe Williams from Good Sam. Stayed all night in Capt. Miller's room.

January 21, Friday, 1944

Signed in post. Maj. Anderson visited. Worked 11-7 on cardiac wd. Sent Moe a telegram. Received mail & moved into room afer washing hair & receiving his telegram with the good news.

January 22, Saturday, 1944

Worked till 1:00. Took cab with other kids & made round trip with Peggy Knox. The train was ½ hour late, he was standing there waiting for me, we stood & talked & then I called Peggy & was going to tell her I was not coming back Sunday and was going to ride back with a nurse from 35th. Then we walked everywhere with the suitcase trying to get rooms & got caught in the rain. Finally settled, then cleaned up & went to the Blue Cross room then had Bar BQ'd steaks & French fries. Then went to the Platinum room & danced. Had a swell time & wonderful night, he was so nice to me.

January 23, Sunday 1944

Had breakfast. Tried to miss the train, just hated, hated to leave & finally we had to run for it. He was so swell. Got back at Billings exhausted. Got mail & a compact from Riles & worked 1-7 with Knox. Dashed off duty to get dressed to go to the hockey game with 11 others. Went on bus. It was good. We lost. They're all Canadians. Had trouble getting home, buses packed. Called cab & then we had a flat tire. It's going to be dull here.

January 24, Monday, 1944

Had a 1:00 off. Rode with kids to get O.D.'s & discovered I couldn't have them cause I didn't have papers. Slept in afternoon & washed & cleaned & wrote letters in the evening. Very dull social life I guess but nice patients.

January 25, Tuesday, 1944

Worked 7-12 & 4-7. Looked around on 1116 & I'm the head nurse there. Sgt. Wards pt. proposed tonight. Was fitted for O.D.'s today in afternoon & saw "What a Woman." It was good.

January 26, Wednesday, 1944

Worked 7-1. Nice patients. Slept in afternoon. Went to see special service woman who wants me to speak. Letter from Moe, Dottie & home. Wrote letters then went bowling with Schultz & Mullens & several officers – kept score.

January 27, Thursday, 1944

Started on 1116 as head nurse. Worked 7-1 & had fun with the boys. Had some patients overseas. Went to town with Schultz & Anne & shopped around. Went to the Off. Club for a cake – had dinner at the cottage & then home. Washed hair & clothes & bought Ovaltine for the kids & fixed up my room. Wrote letters. This place is even more dead than AGN.

January 28, Friday, 1944

Worked 7-9 & 1-7. Cleaned room etc. from 9-1 & worked hard. Wrote letters in the evening.

January 29, Saturday, 1944

Received 3 wonderful letters from Moe. One from home. Then went to movie with Schultz & Anne.

January 30, Sunday, 1944

Beautiful day. Worked 7-1. Slept, read, washed & wrote letters – dull part of my life.

January 31, Monday, 1944

2 sweet letters & Valentine from Moe. He really wants me to come to Louisville again & wanted me this weekend. Says he's not going to write Vicki anymore. Worked hard – wrote letters in the evening. Gully, I want so much to get into the 107th.

February 1, Tuesday, 1944

17 months in the Army. Worked 7-3. Like duty now on 1116 & Capt. Fernburg is nice. Received sweet letter from Moe. 2nd one he'd written on Sunday. Went to movie with kids & saw "Song of Russia" – Superb. Really felt I was seeing it with him.

February 2, Wednesday, 1944

Started new pool of nurses on our wd. Enjoy duty. Sent Moe a telegram since he wants me to come. Wrote letters in the evening. Received pictures from DeLucia.

February 3, Thursday, 1944

Worked & wrote letters. Received a nazi flag from Hebel.

February 4, Friday, 1944

Received 2 letters from him from Wed. Vicki ditched him again. She is heartless. I can't understand her. One special delivery & the telegram. Stayed in and got ready.

February 5, Saturday, 1944

Worked till 12:00. Went in on train with another girl as far as Jeffersonville. I got there first. Brown couldn't take us in, split up reservations so went to Victoria's. Was so glad to see him & he got in an awful lot of trouble. Takes Vicki incident very well. Had supper & Bar BQ & went to the plantation room & danced. Had a wonderful time. He really is a swell swell guy & so sweet to me. I wouldn't be so surprised if we got together yet. I feel so sorry for him & like him so much.

February 6, Sunday, 1944

Slept late, then went to French village & had chicken. Read funnies & listened to the radio. Took pictures, drank O.J. & had hot dog. Went to old double feature with Nancy Carroll & held hands & ate popcorn. Ate steak & French fries at Bar BQ & he bought me a darling pin & was so very very sweet. I really like him & I know he likes me among others. Felt very funny when his train pulled out at 9:30. I went to U.S.O. until 11:30. Got home at 3:00 after cab ride & found N.N. sign on my door.

February 7, Monday, 1944

Worked 7-12 on 1116 & looked over 1102, 1100 & 1101. Got special delivery from Moe & a letter from MacDowell, Bessler, a long one he wants to visit me on leave & from home. Wasn't sleepy at all first night. Wrote letters.

February 8, Tuesday, 1944

Had fun with patients & wrote letters. N.D. (night duty)

February 9, Wednesday, 1944

Same. Nothing new or different – N.D. Nice patients.

February 10, Thursday, 1944

Same. N.D.

February 11, Friday, 1944

Same. Like N.D. Called home.

February 12, Saturday, 1944

Same. Wish it was last week.

February 13, Sunday, 1944

Nothing unusual.

February 14, Monday, 1944

9 letters all together. Darling Valentine from Broch. 3 letters from Moe & they're leaving.

February 15, Tuesday, 1944

Got pictures – pretty good.

February 16, Wednesday, 1944
No entry.

February 17, Thursday, 1944
No entry.

February 18, Friday, 1944
No entry.

February 19, Saturday, 1944

Met Ruth May in town & had supper at the cottage & then out on bus. She went on duty with me & Lt. Street said it was ok if she stayed on duty & she talked with my corps non-student who walked us off duty to Maj. Anderson's door & she came out & was ready to tear me to pieces, she was so mad. Lt. Street tried to console me when I told them – never a 1st now even a head nurse even if age didn't count.

February 20, Sunday, 1944

Went to see Maj. Anderson to explain. She was still furious & hates me. Slept till 2:00 with Ruth May then she & I went to town & ate in balcony of drug store & then went to a part of a show & I put her on bus. Poor kid still worried & me too. Told him about it. Moe called me from N.Y. at 11:30 & we talked till 11:45. He is wonderful & told me he thinks I'm the sweetest most wonderful girl in the world & was upset & worried about the letter I wrote him about Marilyn & told me I would have made the same hit she did.

February 21, Monday, 1944
No entry.

February 22, Tuesday, 1944

Had impacted wisdom tooth pulled & Capt. Russell & Maj. Anderson were there.

February 23, Wednesday, 1944
No entry.

February 24, Thursday, 1944
No entry.

February 25, Friday, 1944
Betty Jean phoned me.

February 26, Saturday, 1944
Nothing unusual.

February 27, Sunday, 1944
Got up at 3:30 & met Betty Jean Wigson – Hebel's girl at 3:30. We went for a ride & told each other everything, reminisced – she adored Bob & gave me a snapshot of him. She's cute & nice but she was a little jealous of me.

February 28, Monday, 1944
Have nice cute patients.

February 29, Tuesday, 1944
Rosemary Mcgrine is here and awakened me, pleasantly surprised, took her to P.O. & I met Capt. Reissmann along the way. He came up on the Wd. in the evening & we had a reunion.

MEMORANDA

Good month – much happier. Had been receiving mail from Moe. Rosemary is here – met Capt. Reissmann again from ship.

Have a swell bunch of patients. Been a pleasure taking care of them. Cutey 1st Lt. Dwight Kennedy from 8th Air Force – England.

March 1, Wednesday, 1944

Kennedy stayed in – fuse burned out – sick pt. Lt. not sick but precautionary medic infection from post mortem getting penicillin. Finished "Here is Your War". Ernie Pyle N. Africa. Wonderful. Gave it to Kennedy to return.

March 2, Thursday, 1944

Letter from Bresler again. Pretty busy. Kennedy came in early & sat & talked & we planned his & my pass so that he could try and meet me in Cincy. He was very cute but sleepy – raises his eyebrow is the 3rd one who does that now = Bob, Moe & now Kennedy.

March 3, Friday, 1944

Usual night – fun with patients. Not as busy as past few nights. Kennedy stayed in, just went to movie. Got his 3 days & took address & both phone numbers, is going to try and make it. Will send telegram Thursday night. Said good bye. Wrote letters. He said I should plan for steaks.

March 4, Saturday, 1944

Usual enjoyable night & duty.

March 5, Sunday, 1944

Nothing unusual.

March 6, Monday, 1944

Got off & got ready and left at 9:00 & got 10:00 am bus. Teamed down all the way & got home about 2:00 pm. Took a cab & had a nice visit with the family but went to sleep at 7:00 pm.

March 7, Tuesday, 1944

Slept late. Went with mom to visit Aunt Etta at Beth's. Came home for supper & then we went to see Tommy Dorsey. Got telegram from Kennedy. Couldn't make it.

March 8, Wednesday, 1944

Washed my hair, then Ruth May & I went to town & had our pictures & I had my feet fixed etc. Then came home & packed. Johnny came over for a while. The family put me on a 7:30 bus ride back with soldiers who invited me to his house Sat. for a party. Got home about 1:00 am. Tired & cold.

March 9, Thursday, 1944

Started as head nurse on 120 north. Nice wd. Had a 1-5 off & Kennedy called at 3:30 said he'd phoned twice the night before & planned to meet me at 7:45. He was late because he went to town after "The Red Charger" his coupe. Lt. Little tried to get him drunk, he got here at 8:10 & we had a wonderful ride, crazy one into town & saw "Jane Eyre" – he's a cute swell kid & lots of fun. Stopped for hamburgers & coffee & got lost coming home. Beautiful night. Got in at 2:00am. He's trying to postpone his leave and has big plans for us.

March 10, Friday, 1944

Worked 7-1. Cute patients, almost all Sgts. staff & tech. Nice Ward. Rode into town on bus with Lt. Hoffman & met Betty Jean at bus station. Went to the athletic club for a delicious buffet supper & orchestra, talked & then stopped at Parkmoor & she brought me home early because I was tired.

March 11, Saturday, 1944

Worked 7-1 today. Worked & got Ward spic & span for inspection. Waited & waited for Kennedy to come over. Then went off duty & drilled – wakened Rosemary & went to the P.O. PX – received another absolutely, crazy letter from Bob, practically a proposal this time. Discovered Kennedy went on 3-day pass which made me a little peeved but I guess it was for a reason. Stayed in, listened to the radio & wrote letters.

March 12, Sunday, 1944

Wrote letters. Went on duty 1-7. Not busy, just messed around all afternoon then came off & got Campbell to go to hockey game with gang of us. Our seats were separated & we waited and waited for a cab in the Parkmoor. "The Red Charger" was in the parking lot when we got in at 11:30.

March 13, Monday, 1944

Beautiful day. Kennedy came up on Ward & stayed till Capt. Weinstein came & after acting silly had to dash away. He & Lt. Campbell are going to speak tonight in town. I stayed in and wrote letters & washed my hair etc.

March 14, Tuesday, 1944

Worked 7-9 & 1-7. Went to PX with kids at noon. Maj. Anderson told me she had been looking for me to give a speech but couldn't find me. Kennedy came up on the Wd about 5. Met him at 8:30 & we went for a ride with the roof down, it was a beautiful warm night. Got gas & rode through town then country then got a Bar BQ at the Tee Pee drive in. He's fun & entertaining. When I came in had a birthday callegram from Moe.

March 15, Wednesday, 1944

Worked 7-1. Kennedy didn't come up or call – he's a crazy guy, can't figure him out. Stayed in and went to bed early.

March 16, Thursday, 1944

Worked 7-1 & 5-7. Had fun with the pool officers – one tall cute one I met on N.D. comes to see Capt. Nelson. Stayed in.

March 17, Friday, 1944

Now I'm head nurse of both 1202 & 1203 – pretty busy & falling over pool officers. Kennedy came up on the Ward again as I was reading the Fire Registrations & he was caught between all the pool Wd Surg's & Lt. Dirkwood, the result he just took off again. Phoned in afternoon & said he had to go shopping. Worked in evening. Convoy came in.

March 18, Saturday, 1944

Worked 7-9 & 1-7. Missed out on inspection, thank goodness – 2 Wards to worry about. Kennedy was up in the morning & came back in the afternoon with a friend who came in on the convoy last night from his squadron. Conner wanted me to go to movies in town with them but I stayed home & wrote to Bresler & read.

March 19, Sunday, 1944

Stayed in and cleaned & washed everything including furniture & clothes I could get my hands on. Rearranged my room & wrote letters. Terrible cold. Rosemary comes off nights tomorrow.

March 20, Monday, 1944

Worked 7-1 & 5-7. Fun morning. 2 Wards cute new 1st Lt. MD on 1203 wouldn't mind a date with. Rode down with Rosemary on bus with Capt. Reismann & Lt. friend of his. Met several other officers we knew. I bought a raincoat & we met Kennedy & had fun waiting for Eileen R.M. & then Kennedy drove us home. Guess he really isn't married. Said he was up on Ward but couldn't find me.

March 21, Tuesday, 1944

Worked 7-1 & went to town with Rosemary & Eileen – shopped for uniforms, ate in canary cottage & then met Betty Jean & we saw "Thousands Cheer." She drove us home early after we shopped at the Tee Pee.

March 22, Wednesday, 1944

Worked 7-1 & 5-7. Received another 2 darling sweet letters from Bob Bresler, he means business but can't make it this weekend. Stayed in & answered him etc.

March 23, Thursday, 1944

Worked 7-1 & came off & wrote letters. Intended to stay home but Jeane Campbell asked me to go on a double date with her with 2 intern medics. Tall, nice & fun – Lt. Furlong I was with & she with Lt. Hargrove. Rode bus to bingo at Officers club. Gobs of fun but we won nothing. They had to hold up the bus for us. Wore my OD's for first time. He asked me to go to the symphony Sunday but I'm going home.

March 24, Friday, 1944

Worked 7-1 & 5-7. Phoned home & Mom and Dad received an anniversary card from Moe. Stayed in & cleaned & washed my hair etc.

March 25, Saturday, 1944

Worked 7-1. Capt. Miller called & said I couldn't get my day off. Dashed downtown & it rained, bought mom and dad each a gift. Ruth May & DeLucia met me at Rose Road & oh what a reunion. We had supper then talked, danced & decorated cellar. Then at 10:30 drove us down & we put DeLucia on the train.

March 26, Sunday, 1944

Got 5:30 bus & slept most of the way. Worked 1-7 & stayed in in the evening.

March 27, Monday, 1944

Worked 7-1 & took a nap then wrote 7 letters. Read & went to bed early. Got birthday card from Moe. First I've heard.

March 28, Tuesday, 1944

Worked 7-9 & 1-7. Received letter from home, Gulmon, Mrs. Neumann, Stars and Stripes & 3 first delicious letters from Moe from Ireland. He's so very sweet – haven't heard from Bresler for a while. Can't understand why. Stayed in & read & wrote letters.

March 29, Wednesday, 1944

Nothing unusual happened.

March 30, Thursday, 1944

Worked splits & had inspections from Wash. DC – stayed over. Rosemary's trying to get in touch with Bresler. Letter from Moe. Nothing unusual. To bed.

March 31, Friday, 1944

What a day! Sealscoth & Stevens had all ready asked if I could move in quarters #2. Moved & it's wonderful. While moving Bob Bresler called & is coming Monday 4:00pm, then Maj. Anderson came in & said she forgave the enlisted men incident & will put me in for promotion – wow 3 in a row. Dashed to town and met Rosemary, Eileen & her girlfriend had supper, shopped & had my photo taken & went to movie and then saw Eileen to the station & took cab home with several other officers.

MEMORANDA

Ended as quite a favorable month. Things always seem to look up in the spring. Gradually I'm slowly getting over the hurt & just wonder what the rest of this year will hold. Rosemary's sis Eileen was here & is a cute kid. Don't know what I'd do without Rosemary, it's a comfort knowing she's here. Didn't hear from Moe too much. Enjoy Ward much more than usual. Capt. Paris said Maj. Fischer told him he knows me @ Knox & I was efficient?? Wonder what Bresler friendship brings forth & sometimes I'm pretty much convinced he'd like to marry me.

April 1, Saturday, 1944

Worked 7-9 and 1-7. Cleaned up place for inspection which they said was better. Told Maj. Anderson it would be at least a week before I could get the pictures. Washed clothes, hair & wrote letter to Moe.

April 2, Sunday, 1944

Worked 7-1. Slept & read in afternoon. Nothing special at all, just anticipating tomorrow.

April 3, Monday, 1944

Worked 7-1. Just was expecting something to happen. Received Bob's telegram telling me his leave was not approved, boy was I mad. The doctors all had a time with me. Well I guess it's for his own good. Received 4 V-mail written on ship from Moe & one from DeLucia. Wrote letters & read.

April 4, Tuesday, 1944

Worked 7-1 & 5-7. Nothing unusual at all.

April 5, Wednesday, 1944

Worked 7-1. Got a sweet letter from Moe again. Stayed in & read & messed around. Rosemary & I decided it was a waste of time going to town.

April 6, Thursday, 1944

Worked 7-1 & 4-7. Had fun with crazy patients double talking & nice
pool officer Lt. Monahan who keeps wanting to take me out but he's
married. Received letters from Bob & he was in fight at Officer's club
& got into trouble, that's why his leave was not approved. Stayed in –
reading "A Tree Grows in Brooklyn." Good.

April 7, Friday, 1944

"Good Friday" Pored down raining all day. Worked 7-1. Lt. Monahan
still heckling. Rosuemary & I each wanted a date with Lt. Costello.
Strange I should meet him in the hall 3 times. Once he was going to get
me & I felt jittery & he backed away & said we'd hope to get together
since we're both assigned here. Could find no one to go to church with
me so I stayed home & cleaned & washed & read the Bible.

April 8, Saturday, 1944

Worked 7-1 & Rosemary & I were to get ride home, shopped, missed
them, bus etc. Ended up going home on train. Family met us. Had fun
just with family, they're so sweet, gave them & Gramma Easter presents.
Visited grandparents.

April 9, Sunday, 1944

Went to church – Easter Sunday. Had fun at home – just adore my
family. Went to Aunt Freda's for supper. Gang all there including
soldiers. Had Easter egg hunt etc. Tech students came after us & we got
ride back. Nice time.

April 10, Monday, 1944

Received card from Bresler from Memphis & he was on his way home,
crazy guy, he was disgusted & sorry he said. Guess that's the end of that,
he hadn't received either of my 2 letters. Worked 7-9 & 1-7. It rained.
Stayed in & wrote letters etc.

April 11, Tuesday, 1944

Worked 7-1. Went to town with Rosemary & picked up the pictures &
returned Daddy's shirt. Went to show & Henry Aldrich on stage.

April 12, Wednesday, 1944

Worked 7-10 & went to luncheon at Marriott Hotel with Rosemary & Mrs. Huff from R.C. – her husband is running for congressman & they're big shots. 2 sons George & Al, she took us to her home & treated us swell. We each sparked a few words. They gave us flowers & hankies. Talked to Peg, nurse from the Pacific. Had the blues in the evening after Maj. Anderson told me my pictures weren't satisfactory.

April 13, Thursday, 1944

Worked 7-1. Capt. Reismann is going to be our Wd. Surgeon. Read "A Tree Grows in Brooklyn" & washed my hair. Put it up in Rosemary's room & Rita Offerle read poetry to us. Called home & told them not to pay any attention to my letter.

April 14, Friday, 1944

Wish this was last year. Worked 7-1. Nothing happened.

April 15, Saturday, 1944

Worked 7-9 & 1-7. Quite different than last year. Stayed in and had the blues.

April 16, Sunday, 1944

Worked 7-1 & then showed cadet nurse around hospital. Took them on my Wards. Then went to town with Sealsect & brothers & had supper at Seville & saw "Tender Comrade." Sad.

April 17, Monday, 1944

Worked 7-9 & 1-7. Stayed in & read etc. Nothing exciting. Was going to town with Rosemary but too tired. Lt. Monahan was going to look for us. Received Moe's V-mail upon landing. Betty Jane phoned.

April 18, Tuesday, 1944

Worked 7-1 & 5-7. Lt. Monahan still insists I go with him, said his wife even gave permission after he told her about me. I am lonely and do want to go out & then former cute patient from Indiana in Bloomington called & wanted to know why I couldn't go to dance with him. Helps morale knowing I'm wanted even tho' impossible situations, both cute. Wrote letters.

April 19, Wednesday, 1944

Worked 7-1 & received 2 sweet letters from Moe, one with clippings about Easter bonnet & the other with a green hanky. Also received a card from Kennedy saying he'd be back to haunt me soon. Went to town with Rosemary & then to movie, saw "Chip Off the Old Block."

April 20, Thursday, 1944

Worked 7-1 & 4-7. Kids were in a parade. Nothing special happened. Stayed in instead of going to get acquainted party at the club. I washed hair, cleaned room etc.

April 21, Friday, 1944

Worked 7-1. Received letters from home, Ralph Messmore, DeLucia & Hebel. Beautiful day again. Stayed in cause Rosemary's on call & haven't seen Kennedy yet.

April 22, Saturday, 1944

Had a 1:00 off & Rosemary & I shopped & came home early. Had chance to go to the dance but didn't think it was worth while. Rosemary went & got drunk.

April 23, Sunday, 1944

Worked 7-1 – phoned Betty Jane & she, Rosemary & I went for a ride then stopped at her apartment & met her mom & her girlfriend. Then she came to my room with me & read Hebel's letter.

April 24, Monday, 1944

Nothing special happened.

April 25, Tuesday, 1944

Worked split till 7. Enjoyed Ward pts. & doctors & all. Went to town with Rosemary & we saw "Women Courageous."

April 26, Wednesday, 1944

Worked 7-1 & then went back at 6:00. Lt. Dukowich said I didn't
have to stay. Had fun in the morning with crazy Lt. Monahan & Capt.
Reismann. Saw Kennedy talking to 2 nurses, guess he & his friend were
taking them out. Guess our little friendship is over. I was more mad than
hurt cause of card & everything.

April 27, Thursday, 1944

Nothing unusual. Went to town, didn't get much done.

April 28, Friday, 1944

Dull day as usual.

April 29, Saturday, 1944

Worked 7-9 & 1-7. Went on double date with Helen Street. My date,
dentist Lt. Dick Kuhlman was married but young, cute, nice & fun.
Danced at the club – formal.

April 30, Sunday, 1944

Worked 7-1 – messed around in the afternoon. As I was in the tub Lt.
Monahan phoned, then called back and said there were complications, if
I'd go to the movie he'd explain later so we double dated & saw movie.
Then went to the club for beer & pretzels – had fun. He was teasing me
all night.

MEMORANDA

No memo's, only fairly blue & lonely month. Awful compared with last
year.

May 1, Monday, 1944

Worked 7-3, went to lecture then dressed & went to town after supper &
shopped. Then to movie "Up in Arms." Got home very late.

May 2, Tuesday, 1944

Worked 7-1 & 4-7. Had usual fun with pts. Monahan asked me to go out again but I wouldn't do it much as I wanted to. Stayed in washed hair, clothes etc. To bed early. Marian O'Drisell was here to see pts. on Ward.

May 3, Wednesday, 1944

Worked 7-1. Took sun bath in side yard in bathing suits. Had cramps after supper – stayed in. It stormed & rained in evening.

May 4, Thursday, 1944

Worked 7-1 & 4-7. V-mail again from Moe. Said good bye to Monahan he is so cute & funny, he & Reismann are nuts. Hate to see him leave & will miss him. Hacker was telling me at supper Kennedy asked about me & is rather disgusted about himself, poor kid, guess that's why I haven't heard or seen him. Feel better about it. Stayed in & wrote letters.

May 5, Friday, 1944

Received telegram – kids will be coming tomorrow to visit. Stayed in & cleaned.

May 6, Saturday, 1944

Worked 7-1 & Rosemary & I met Ruth May & Marilyn at train station & settled them at The Columbia Club & then took them to the Seville to eat. Rode to circus but didn't stay. Came back into town & saw "Mark Twain." It was late when Rosemary & I finally reached comp.

May 7, Sunday, 1944

Worked 7-1 & Rosemary & Marilyn were here & we rode into town on bus and walked around & chatted & got a sandwich then I put them on train & came back to comp alone.

May 8, Monday, 1944

Worked 7-9 & 1-7. Not a thing exciting or unusual happened. Quite, quite different from last year this date when I just begin to live.

May 9, Tuesday, 1944

Lt. Monahan was up & said good bye. He left today. Nothing special happened.

May 10, Wednesday, 1944

Not a thing exciting or unusual happened. Very dull in comparison to last year.

May 11, Thursday, 1944

Went to town with Cookie & Rosemary.

May 12, Friday, 1944

Worked 7-1. Had inspection & passed. Very hot in afternoon. Stafford said Stern was going to ask me to a dance at 812th but I told them all I was not dating our officers. Went to show. Lots of chances to go to parties again & dates galore to go to our dance but stayed in & wrote letters. Rice told me she & Capt. Bell saw us last night & she likes Rodenbough very much. I really hope he waits for me for 2 weeks & I kinda think he will but you can't tell.

May 13, Saturday, 1944

Worked 7-1 & spent the afternoon trying to cash Moe's check, finally got train home & met Snabel & Alering on train, they offered me part of their seats & Daddy met me at the train. Spent a quiet evening home.

May 14, Sunday, 1944

Went to church, fist time home in O.D.'s. Alma came home for dinner. Pitched horseshoes & played with Bonnie. In evening danced & Charles threw me over his head in true jitter bug style. They all saw me off at the train station & I kissed them all good bye. Finally sat between soldiers from Ottersburg.

May 15, Monday, 1944

Worked 7-1 & 5-7. Went to QM for O.D. issue. Received cute letter from Lt. Monahan. Washed hair & cleaned room etc.

May 16, Tuesday, 1944

Worked 7-4:30. We were very busy therefore didn't do much in the evening. Put up my hair etc.

May 17, Wednesday, 1944

No entry.

May 18, Thursday, 1944

No entry.

May 19, Friday, 1944

No entry.

May 20, Saturday, 1944

No entry.

May 21, Sunday, 1944

No entry.

May 22, Monday, 1944

No entry.

May 23, Tuesday, 1944

No entry.

May 24, Wednesday, 1944

No entry.

May 25, Thursday, 1944

Went to Pond theater with Veremko, started to walk home & got a ride in a convertible with 5 enlisted men.

May 26, Friday, 1944

Had a 1 off & Veremko & I went bike riding & went to PX (Main) swell. Had fun. In evening went riding to PX again to get cakes & food for kids. Keller gave me a feather bob.

May 27, Saturday, 1944

Worked 7-9 & 1-7. Had trouble getting ready but finally got Veremko ready & she, Scott & Martin & myself went to town & could have had a bit of fun at the Long Indiana Roof but we didn't stay long enough.

May 28, Sunday, 1944

Had a 1 off. Went to town with Ring & Veremko & saw Henry Bruce. Received pictures from Cpl. He'd taken on barge at Bizerte.

May 29, Monday, 1944

Had a 9-1 off. Got a very long letter from Neumann with his picture. Stayed in.

May 30, Tuesday, 1944

Betty Jane phoned & talked & cried & carried on for at least ½ hour. Said she's through with Hebel etc. cause she gets V-mail & I get long letter.

May 31, Wednesday, 1944

Betty Jane phoned & apologized & wants me to come down. I went down to her aptmt. & her letters have changed & that's cause he has "but it's" because he stopped loving her.

June 1, Thursday, 1944

Went to movie with Cookie and saw "Hitler Gang." It was very good.

June 2, Friday, 1944

Nothing special happened. Had usual fun with patients.

June 3, Saturday, 1944

Worked 7-1 & got 5 o'clock train home. Had fun with some nice kids, one cute Sgt. who was visiting cousin in Mt. Adams & arranged to get 11:55 train. Went home in evening after Daddy met me & just visited family.

June 4, Sunday, 1944

Slept late instead of going to church. Alma came for dinner. Priscilla drove us down as Daddy came later to Aunt Freda's. Gang there, bunch of strange girls, wore my beige suit & they all took me to the station. Met darling Sgt. Cousin & then he came up later as we planned to meet, rode back together but didn't get to sit together.

June 5, Monday, 1944

Worked split. Have cute patients. Felt sick, nauseated & very nervous in evening. Went to bed early.

June 6, Tuesday, 1944

"D-Day" Was awakened this morning by radio news broadcasts & the ringing of the Liberty Bell from Phil. – D-Day started at mm over there this morning. Chills & tears & strange, left out nauseated feeling over my reaction. Worked 7-1 & all the fellows wish they were back over. News broadcasts all day. Stayed home in evening to write letters. If only I'd get orders.

June 7, Wednesday, 1944

No entry.

June 8, Thursday, 1944

No entry.

June 9, Friday, 1944

Worked late. Nothing special happened. Met Alma at the bus station at 10:00 pm. Got her situated at the Washington hotel & then had gobs of fun on the bus with officers who started to sing & then we all sang all the way home at the end they serenaded us at the quarter.

June 10, Saturday, 1944

Worked 7-1 & rushed down to meet Alma & get her from Washington hotel & managed to get another room at the Severin where I'm going to have to stay with her. Then met Scott & Verenko & we messed around then movie. Scott left & Verenko stayed with us too. Had fun. Got up at 5:00 am. Bus at 6:00 am.

June 11, Sunday, 1944

Worked 7-1. After dinner Verenko & I took Alma out Riverside & met some enlisted men, we talked to & we had to push our way on bus with girl. They took us on all the rides, roller coasters etc. & then went to town with us & helped us get Alma on bus. Had a lot of fun.

June 12, Monday, 1944

Worked split 9-1 off. In evening Verenko & I went to Coliseum for 1st Bond drive show. Lt. Bill Holden, Donald O'Conner & air corps, Bond (Glen Miller). Got a ride home on special bus to Ft. Harrington & had fun singing & harmonizing all the way. Rode down on bus.

June 13, Tuesday, 1944

Worked 7-1 – nothing special happened. Capt. Reismann had the afternoon off & I think he wanted to ask me to go out but some how he's bashful or something. Went swimming with the kids, it was cold. Sang all the way home on bus.

June 14, Wednesday, 1944

Worked split hours & worked late. Had fun with patients & Capt. Reismann, putting 2 boys on traction. Costello came up to get him to eat steak but he worked late & made me omelet for supper. Thought for sure he'd ask me for the dance, he hinted so much, told the boys he'd take me to the Ind. Roof & dance off any wgt. they'd put on me etc. Stayed in in the evening.

June 15, Thursday, 1944

Bombed Japan. Worked 7-1. Capt. Reismann came in early & thought
he'd ask me then but the pts. came around so he put on casts & then
Verenko met me & we went down the romp & met Capt. Reismann &
I said I wanted him this morning cause of eggs & he said how about
going on a date with him tonight & I messed with him & ignored him &
Verenko could have killed me. Then he asked if I was off when & when
I'd be back. Stayed in.

June 16, Friday, 1944

Had a 1-4 off. Thought for sure Capt. Reismann would ask me but he
didn't. Stayed in and wrote letters.

June 17, Saturday, 1944

No entry.

June 18, Sunday, 1944

No entry.

June 19, Monday, 1944

No entry.

June 20, Tuesday, 1944

Saw good movie "Going My Way." Got ride home in Jeep.

June 21, Wednesday, 1944

Reismann asked me to go to their picnic & said I was going if he had to
carry me.

June 22, Thursday, 1944

Reismann really wanted me to go to Lt. Swanke's picnic but it was
rained out. Worked late instead with penicillin & blood transfers. He
fixed my omelets on the Ward.

June 23, Friday, 1944

Had a 1 off & went with Verenko to meet Purky. Took her to the Seville & then to movie. Nothing exciting. Several more letters from Moe.

June 24, Saturday, 1944

Had a 11-3 off. Guess Reismann didn't ask me cause Costello came. He asked me if I was going. Stayed in. Scottie went to dance with Reatin & danced all night with Barclay.

June 25, Sunday, 1944

Had a 1 off. Went to town with Verenko & her girlfriend. Had very pleasant surprise of meeting Capt. Gabin, Reilly & Fred Cooper who are down here for the infiltration course. Then went to Riverside & came down to movie then put her on train.

June 26, Monday, 1944

Had a 9-1 off. Kocher told me Don McClough was here too & was going to call. Nothing special happened except Capt. Reismann asked me to play golf with him. Stayed in & wrote letters.

June 27, Tuesday, 1944

Nothing special. Capt. Reismann told me he sent my picture home to his dad cause his dad knows me. Rode to swimming pool with Schultz, saw everybody.

June 28, Wednesday, 1944

Worked till noon, then went on nights on 1100 & 1101 & 2. Good ole same Wards. Lt. Sawnker knew my name & all about me apparently from Reismann. Was busy & all ate together in pts. mess.

June 29, Thursday, 1944

Don came down on the Ward & we really had a reunion & reminisced for about 2 hours. He suggested we write. Schultz told me Reismann was going to ask me to the dorm.

June 30, Friday, 1944

Nothing special.

July 1, Saturday, 1944

Verenko went to dance with Hordle & Scottie with Barclay. Had fun with patients & students.

July 2, Sunday, 1944

Slept late & well after Verenko told me Reismann didn't go to the dance. He & Lt. were O.D. & told me of my promotion coming through & asked me to go to Brooklyn with him if I could have had a leave. Was sweet & came back later but didn't stay. Can't figure him.

July 3, Monday, 1944

Walked off with Reismann, met him in the Hall & he loaned me $31.00. Slept all day. Got letter from Hebel & Moe. Hebel was sweet as usual & they're near 3rd General.

July 4, Tuesday, 1944

Really enjoy night duty down on those 3 Wards. Several cute patients I have fun with.

July 5, Wednesday, 1944

Slept then worked & nothing special happened. Then Capt. Barclay & Lindell suggested it would be fun to get a picnic & I should try and get a note for the Capt. They are very swell to me & lots of fun.

July 6, Thursday, 1944

Made arrangements with Verenko & Captain & Don after they came back from the club. They even bought tuna fish. Think it will be fun.

July 7, Friday, 1944

Slept till noon. Wore slacks and silk shirt. Don Lindell was out there yelling for me to get on the ball at 1:30. Verenko went with Capt. Berkley. Went to driving range then Broad Ripple, swimming, horse fights & took pictures. Then went shopping in Piggly Wiggly store & Don was so darling, pushed the basket around & brought everything. Went back to Broad Ripple for picnic, then nice ride back. When we got back discovered kids had orders for CJ Ellis. Such excitement. Good day.

July 8, Saturday, 1944

Nothing exceptional happened.

July 9, Sunday, 1944

Stayed up & went to church & Don played Eddie Dickens theme song &
then one more for me. Met him later & walked down the romp with him.
He's a doll. The kids left for Ellis – Scotty & Verenko.

July 10, Monday, 1944

Washed my hair. Don Gulmon called from town, he had a lay-over on his
way home. Good to see him. Went to James Whiteman room & talked.
Then to double feature & had to say good bye. Don got his orders & is
mad about it. So he stayed up & we talked till after 3 about everything
under the sun & he told me about his family.

July 11, Tuesday, 1944

Slept till Don called me & wanted me to go swimming & on another
picnic but I slept instead. Had fun on duty. He's so sweet – no students
at night again. Didn't go to night supper. Don walked me over & got my
Bobby pins & we planned tomorrow, sure hate to see him go.

July 12, Wednesday, 1944

Don called me at 8:30, rode down on bus. Inquired as to time in bus
station. Took cab to train station & bought tickets for Cincy. Station man
insisted we must be carried. He phones Coffman & got permission to
stay, be there at 8:30 tomorrow. Ate at Wheelers & then went to double
feature then back to train station. I tried to call home. Got train, I dozed,
he ate & Daddy & Mrs. Marsh met us at train. Then we went home
for supper, then to get Ruth May. Rode to Coney, went on all the rides.
Then danced at Moonlite Gardens & rode to get his sentence at terminal
& then bus station where he & Daddy were.

July 13, Thursday, 1944

Slept till 5pm. Had supper & visited Robertses & Gramma & Grandpa's.
Then went down to bus station. Sure wished Don was there to come
back with me. Got 10:30 bus & arrived at 2:00. Got ride in cab with our
enlisted men.

July 14, Friday, 1944

Started to work at H.N. on 1102 & 1103 ENT. Worked 7-9 & 1-7. Nice Wards & patients & WD officers. Capt. Sisko 3rd Gen. Had fun with crazy Lt. Nice. Got nice telegram from Don, he can't make it tomorrow. Stayed in & slept all evening & night.

July 15, Saturday, 1944

Worked 7-11 & 3-7. About 3:30 Lt. Warren Merrill came up to read & discuss Cooley's case. We talked for a while & then I discovered who he was & that he had gone with Patty & Derrick last week. Then he asked me to go to the dance & got 2 more dates. I got Miller & Cookie & he called twice, once on the Ward & once in the quarters. He's the pick of the post & handsome. What luck! Had a wonderful time. Went to Spencers afterWards & did some smoochin.

July 16, Sunday, 1944

Slept late. Worked till 7:00. Stayed in but did nothing much, was too tired.

July 17, Monday, 1944

Worked 7-4 & Delush called on his way home on leave. Received cute letter from Don written just after he got back there. Rosemary, Crook & I went to town and shopped & bought formals. We had fun. Then Coleman & Clarke met us & we saw "White Cliffs of Dover." Good but sad. Went to Tee Pee later. Got in late & was tired. He's cute but just not too much fun. I like Don a lot better.

July 18, Tuesday, 1944

Worked split & went to get uniforms & then came back & saw Jessie, Nelson & Harriet Hilliard. Then in evening went in balcony with Cooke & Capt. Bacon & Lt. Miller etc. but Fire Marshall closed us out & we went to the PX & back up & saw Charlie McCuly with Edgar Bergen show. Very good.

July 19, Wednesday, 1944

Worked 7-4. Very hard trying to get the place straightened out. Stayed in, wrote to Moe & washed my hair.

July 20, Thursday, 1944

Worked split 7-1 & 4-7. Finally getting Ward straightened out. Stayed in to try & catch up on letters & everything in my room. Didn't hear from Don or Merrill yet but don't care if I don't hear from Merrill. Got larger pictures of us & holding my breath to hear from Dan.

July 21, Friday, 1944

Worked 7-3. Had to have our pictures taken again for cards. Discovered letter from Adj. Gen. & I'm a 1st Lt. Got back on Ward & Lt. Nice said Merrill had been up twice & left a number for me to call but he told him I was going home which I verified. Don phoned long distance from Columbus about 6:00 pm, he's going to fly to movie, gosh he's darling, wish I could see more of him. He's going to try & get a few days off but I doubt it.

July 22, Saturday, 1944

Had a 1:00 off. Got a 3:30 bus & home about 8:00am. Alma came down & she & all the family & I went to Weiss's. Had a nice time.

July 23, Sunday, 1944

Got the 9:15 air conditioned train after we took Ruth May to the hospital. Got in Indianapolis at 10:30. Good time. Busy on duty. Really had the blues. Wrote to Hebel & it rained a little.

July 24, Monday, 1944

Worked 7-9 & 1-7. Had cramps. Sorta had the blues all day naturally. We were busy, did a washing in the evening. It rained. Betty Jane called.

July 25, Tuesday, 1944

Took a 9-1 off with Cookie & I did all my ironing. Was busy on the Wards. Nice wd. officers. It rained again practically all day as I knew it would.

July 26, Wednesday, 1944

Worked 7-3. Nice Wards & doctors. Got lots of mail including another letter from Don & card from Capt. Reismann on leave. Stayed in, wrote letters & washed hair.

July 27, Thursday, 1944

Nothing special happened.

July 28, Friday, 1944

Worked till 7 & went for a ride to Wheeler's to eat with Merrill & Cookie & Coleman & Rosemary & Charlie. Had fun, he was nicer, kept wanting to know why I didn't want to go with him, but now he knows better, I have to go home.

July 29, Saturday, 1944

Worked 7-1. Went home & Daddy & Ruth May met me. Mom was at Anne's.

July 30, Sunday, 1944

Got the 9:15 train back from Cincy – rode with 2 other nurses. Worked 1-7 & nothing special happened.

July 31, Monday, 1944

Worked 7-9 & 1-7. Nothing special happened.

MEMORNADA

So glad 1st July is over.

August 1, Tuesday, 1944

Worked 7-3. Lt. Frey, my newest Ward officer left for Breckenridge. Went to main PX with Cookie to get checks cashed. Haven't heard from Don for a while. Wonder if I will? I hope, I hope, I need someone very much.

August 2, Wednesday, 1944

Nothing special.

August 3, Thursday, 1944
Nothing special.

August 4, Friday, 1944
Nothing special.

August 5, Saturday, 1944
Received very cute letter from Bob Reif among others. McIntyre came after Cookie & I had steak supper at Harrison Hotel & then saw "The Unlimited" & went to their home to sleep.

August 6, Sunday, 1944
Slept late then had breakfast with McIntyre & they brought us back. Worked 1-7. 3 letters from Moe in France. 1st ones & wonderful ones.

August 7, Monday, 1944
Finally received sweet letter from Don. Went to town with Gross & Betty Jane who left us.

August 8, Tuesday, 1944
Nothing special. Cookie went with Coleman again.

August 9, Wednesday, 1944
Worked 7-3. Not busy. More mail. Went to early movie with Cookie.

August 10, Thursday, 1944
Worked 7-10 & 2-7. Went to QM with Cookie after the rest of our issue. Got letter from another student & Dottie from France. Stayed home & cleaned.

August 11, Friday, 1944
Worked. Had fun with Stangby & the kids. Got a lot more mail.

August 12, Saturday, 1944

Worked 7-3. Rechtin came over and asked me to go to the dance so I said yes. I wore my new green formal. Went with Lt. Hordke & girl & had pretty good time only he's not a good dancer.

August 13, Sunday, 1944

Worked 7-1. Slept in afternoon & went to "Drive-in" with Rechtin in evening.

August 14, Monday, 1944

Worked 7-3. Went to town with Cookie & shopped for Scotty. Went to Wheelers & met Lt. Steinberg & Lt. Walsh with Hall & we all ate together. Home in cab.

August 15, Tuesday, 1944

Worked split till 7 & went to U.S.O. show in RC yard in evening. Sat with Capt. Wright & Maj. Anderson & wrote letter waiting for it to start.

August 16, Wednesday, 1944

Worked 7-4. Had fun with Lt. Cox & Stangby as usual. He sure is cute. He & S.N. asked me to ride to Cincy with them this weekend. Stayed in, it rained. Lt. Dryer asked me to go to Cincy with him too.

August 17, Thursday, 1944

Had a 4pm off. Nothing special happened. Stayed in.

August 18, Friday, 1944

Lt. Nice asked me to the formal Saturday. Received telegram from Don and he can have 2 days off except Saturday & Sunday.

August 19, Saturday, 1944

Lt. Nice was going home with me & Stangby & Lewis were driving us in Lewis's blue convertible. We were all ready & would have had fun when Lewis was restricted. I went home anyhow & had fun just visiting the family & reading them letters.

August 20, Sunday, 1944

Worked 1-7. Got the 9:15 train after we took R.M. to the hosp. Went to show on post in evening & saw "Two Yanks Abroad." Funny.

August 21, Monday, 1944

Worked till 7. Like my Wards & Lt. Cox, Lt. Nice & Maj. Kreft are nice. Real surprise, got letter from Neumann & he's coming home. Called home & gave them the good news.

August 22, Tuesday, 1944

Nothing special. Worked 7-3. Had a water & cologne fight with Rosemary. Spinal thinks I'm going with them to Paris. Wrote letters. Got letter from Mrs. Neumann & she told me about difference in religion in Ed & his ex. Rostine broke his leg again.

August 23, Wednesday, 1944

Paris was liberated. Worked 7-3 & saw orientation movie 3-4. Got another letter from Don & he's going to try & get 7-9th of September off. He phoned long distance again & he's going to fly away again this weekend. He's being transferred to Dayton.

August 24, Thursday, 1944

No entry.

August 25, Friday, 1944

No entry.

August 26, Saturday, 1944

No entry.

August 27, Sunday, 1944

No entry.

August 28, Monday 1944

No entry.

August 29, Tuesday, 1944
No entry.

August 30, Wednesday, 1944
No entry.

August 31, Thursday, 1944
No entry.

September 1, Friday, 1944
No entry.

September 2, Saturday, 1944
Rode to town with Ball. Buses on strike. Had fun in station with sailors on another truck. Family met me.

September 3, Sunday, 1944
Had fun coming back on train with Sgts. going to Cp. McCoy. Sgt. Gale sat with me. Stayed in.

September 4, Monday, 1944
Lt. Link came down on the Ward & then phoned me but I couldn't talk. We double dated with Lt. Wilson & Lt. Steckle. Went to Sapphire Room & then to "Jonie" then to Tee Pee. Got in at 2:00. Had fun.

September 5, Tuesday, 1944
Worked 7-3. Stayed in.

September 6, Wednesday, 1944
Worked 7-11 & 3-7. The kids say Lt. Link was down looking for me. Wrote Don. Couldn't call him.

September 7, Thursday, 1944

Worked 7-3 36 Ward. Telegram from Don. Couldn't get in touch with him. Wrote letters. Another letter from Hebel, Moe & Neumann. Ed wasn't coming home.

September 8, Friday, 1944

Worked 7-11 & 3-7. Another letter from Don & he really had yesterday & today off. Probably didn't get my telegram, he didn't call. The boys went to Fergie's funeral. Lt. Deyer came over & invited us to go out with him tonight. Helped me do L.P. Stayed in and wrote Don.

September 9, Saturday, 1944

Worked 7-3. Very good news. Don is coming at 6:00 pm. Called me at 5:30. Surprised me. Met him in town & met air corps Capt. & wife in Sapphire Room who invited us to Stout Field club. Had fun dancing. Another couple brought us back. Don slept in Lt. Cox barracks.

September 10, Sunday, 1944

Slept late. Don met me & went on duty with me & was entertained by patients. He played piano as I dressed. Went to town, finally ate at Drug Store, saw Charlie Spiral at Circle. Rushed to bus station & put Don on the train. He's a doll.

September 11, Monday, 1944

Had a PM. Went to town & bought a blue formal.

September 12, Tuesday, 1944

Worked split. Was supposed to go with Dryer but didn't.

September 13, Wednesday, 1944

Worked 7-11 & 3-7. Orders Cp. Kilmer with Mooshy & saw other kids. 10 in all.

September 14, Thursday, 1944

Orders delayed. Got shots.

September 15, Friday, 1944

Got letter from Don. Nothing special happened.

September 16, Saturday, 1944

Worked 7-1 & got ride with Capt. Paris & friend to car line where E.M. helped me then W.O. – carried my boy to the station & met Miller & rode home with her. Got card from Odele Ross & Vincent.

September 17, Sunday, 1944

Made the 9:15 am train back. Worked 1-7. Rostein asked me for a ride. Stayed in & wrote letters.

September 18, Monday, 1944

Worked till 3 am. Cute letter from Neumann. Went to town with Mousley & her girlfriends & saw everyone including Lt. Merrill & Ann Guforth. What a reunion and surprise.

September 19, Tuesday, 1944

Worked 7-3. All the S.N.'s were down & teasing me about Paris. "The Last Time I Saw Paris." Decided to start S.N. Club. Cookie went on leave. Ann was up & we went to see Capt. Reismann.

September 20, Wednesday, 1944

Worked 7-11 & 4-7. Not busy. Nothing unusual happened.

September 21, Thursday, 1944

Nothing unusual. Letters from Don.

September 22, Friday, 1944

Nothing special.

September 23, Saturday, 1944

We had to move the boys to the Wd. & got officers in. Went home & to Weiss's & June gave me a permanent new puppy. Cute.

September 24, Sunday, 1944

Got the 9:15 train & sat with nurses & we were entertained by 2 air corps Lt. Nothing special. Stayed in in evening. Cute S.N.'s. June, Benson etc. were all up.

September 25, Monday, 1944

Moved from 1102 to 1115. Very busy worked 7-6. Went to see movie on Post.

September 26, Tuesday, 1944

Finally getting settled. Good students. Had several other kids come down. Stayed in & washed & stuff.

September 27, Wednesday, 1944

Busy but getting settled. Stan said he's going to have us convinced soon trying to convince them we're going to be married. Strande was in & said we would leave soon. Stayed in.

September 28, Thursday, 1944

Rained. Nothing unusual. Lt. Dryer called & asked me for a date over weekend. Saw show in evening.

September 29, Friday, 1944

Nothing special. Stripped my room to go home.

September 30, Saturday, 1944

Had a 1:00 off. Dashed home on 2:15 train. Daddy picked me up in the U.S.O. Sure wish I had tomorrow off. Storey's home. Weisses were out and that crazy Dryer called 3 times.

October 1, Sunday, 1944

Had to go back on the 9:15. Sat with sailor going home on leave. Worked 7-1 didn't do much.

October 2, Monday, 1944

Worked till 3:00. Went to town & met Lt. Moe & we shopped then she treated me at Claypool where we met Merrill. He was very nice, said he thought I didn't like doctors. Then we had a Bar BQ chicken supper.

October 3, Tuesday, 1944

Worked split. Getting ready.

October 4, Wednesday, 1944

Worked 7-3. Said good bye to my 4 little S.N.'s, Hawkins, Hanson, Jones & Bell. Went to PX & got rid of B. Boys and food lockers. Stayed in & got the rest of my junk together.

October 5, Thursday, 1944

Cleared post in staff car & bid everyone farewell & got set. Kids rode down in cab with Mousley & I & we met the others there. Sgt. of St. Louis, Smith & Turner misses the train & we didn't get one baggage checked but Rassey's boyfriend sent telegram from Columbus for us. Met kids from Attersburg & ate in diner. Talked with 2 new med. Officers & then went back to our car after visiting kids. Mousley had letter from Rosemary for me.

October 6, Friday, 1944

Had breakfast in diner. Nice ride. Got off at New Brunswick when we picked up Turner, Schmidt & all came out in bus together. Messed around. Went to Mess & to PX & had a lot of fun at the Officers Club where we met 8 darling Lts. Had a lot of fun.

October 7, Saturday, 1944

Busy processing. Marched to gas chamber & got lecture with lots of others. March miles everywhere. Then very good lecture on ship.

October 8, Sunday, 1944

Slept late, other kids got shots & we had passes canceled, so saw movie.

October 9, Monday, 1944

Usual rush & marching.

October 10, Tuesday, 1944

Testing all set. Barracks bag & foot lockers finally came & they let us pack a foot locker.

October 11, Wednesday, 1944

More processing. Then dressed & train, band & singing. Beautiful ship. Met Lt. Lavine dental officer in ship. Platoon which brought us back in the Victory Room. Really had a reunion.

October 12, Thursday, 1944

Slept late then H&D groups to orientation meeting in lounge. Running around with Wardsmith. Wrote letters & played cards & met several more officers. Mail from home, Hebel & Moe.

October 13, Friday, 1944

Beautiful day. Boot drill. Usual card playing, letter writing. Song Fest. Sun deck. Saw movie "Standing Room Only."

October 14, Saturday 1944

Usual day. Very warm tho. Nothing exciting – not really like the last time, makes me miss Bob & the kids.

October 15, Sunday, 1944

Went to church. Nothing special only cute air corps in life boat drill. Sat in lounge & played cards.

October 16, Monday, 1944

Had fun with artillery & cavalry playing cards after good movie for which they saved my spot.

October 17, Tuesday, 1944

Wrote letters. U.S.O. show in evening followed by good song fest.

October 18, Wednesday, 1944

Beautiful through field glass (illegible). Played cards all day and in evening. Not so crowded anymore.

Southampton, England

October 19, Thursday, 1944

Had fun. Played cards with the Signal Corp. Lt. He was very nice. Doughnuts and coffee again. Again, seems like old time even if we are cramped. On train in Garvock, Scotland to Southampton, England.

October 20, Friday, 1944

Cramped, stiff & hungry. Walked in rain. Coffee & doughnuts. Terrible bunks but still better than Billings.

October 21, Saturday, 1944

Eating in lounge. Up & around but most of the kids are sick. In evening played cards in saloon. Miserable way to live, cramped.

October 22, Sunday, 1944

Slept through breakfast. Messed around all day & finally made it. Different, exciting & big thrill. Mud & camp fires. Very nice E.M. & officers, finally food then ride & more mud galore.

Arlene second from left.

Paris, France

October 23, Monday, 1944

Rain – mud, mud & more mud. Gathering wood & trying to keep warm.

October 24, Tuesday, 1944

Worked in morning getting wood & digging ditches. Had Sgts. in around our fire to keep warm. In afternoon visited 25th.

October 25, Wednesday, 1944

Nothing special. Went to movie with Chaplain in tent.

October 26, Thursday, 1944

Sandy Goodman was down & came back in evening with Brenda in command car. Went down 25th to visit. Saw everyone, had fun with Biles. They treated me swell, gave me clothes & food. Brought us home again.

October 27, Friday, 1944

Get to go to Paris on D.S.

October 28, Saturday, 1944

Usual day & evening. Sandy Goodman & Maj. came after me to go down the 25th but we went to F.F.I. & Chateau instead. Incredible time.

October 29, Sunday, 1944

Church in field. Packed bedding rolls & got rations. Got ready.

October 30, Monday, 1944

Up at last, then airport. Pilot showed us Paris by air & then rode around on bus & finally Comm. Then 217th bed & food.

October 31, Tuesday, 1944

Slept late. Lunch then had G.I.'s teach us about metro. Went on R.C. Had fun. Got lost, found Cas. Off. Club. Had steak & peach pie. Met boys who knew us.

MEMORANDA

Very glad to be here. I like Paris very much. Wished we could stay.

November 1, Wednesday, 1944

Worked on Wd & to help out. Very busy. Sick boys but nice & fun. Had 2-5 off. Went to PX. After duty went to Wock's livingroom & helped entertain her brother & 3 friends. Fed them rations & cooked them in kitchen. Hope they get back tomorrow. Bedding roll came.

November 2, Thursday, 1944

After breakfast went back up to Wd. Went shopping in a little store across the street with Wocksmith. Had fun on duty. Met Wocksmith's brother & 6 others & took them to our mess. & then after they took us down on the metro, we got lost & finally found St. Augustine, a little American bar then the Cos. Off. Club bar & to 217th truck at 10:30pm. Good cute kids & lots of fun.

November 3, Friday, 1944

Had fun on the Wd changing from French to English beds, like a 3-ring circus. In evening washed hair & clothes.

November 4, Saturday, 1944

Worked till 3:30 & then went shopping with Wocksmith & Turner in shopping dist. around here & went to bed early.

November 5, Sunday, 1944

Worked till 12:30. Went for a sight-seeing walk with the kids & took pictures. Met Donnie & Scanlen from Sig. corps & they took us to look up other outfits then by metro to their mess, after which we went to Cptm. for party. Had swell time. Danced & ended up with Donnie & Bilden, they teased us but he is sweet & decent & I liked him. Came home again.

November 6, Monday, 1944

Got up for meeting. Worked 3-11 and Donnie came up on Ward for a while. He really is cute. Had day off. Went to movie.

November 7, Tuesday, 1944

Worked 3-11. Not busy. Donnie was up 4 times, 8 trips all together. It rained. I met with the crowd after duty till 1:40. He's very cute & an excellent dancer.

November 8, Wednesday, 1944

Worked 11-3. Got hours arranged for tomorrow and Turner is going to work for me. Met Duffey & Capt. Comer & he's going to tell him.

November 9, Thursday, 1944

Evac patients in the AM. Off at 3:30. Got paid at 0800. Donnie came at 5:00 for supper & we picked Duffey up & had chicken. Then went shopping in little stores & then we all piled up the aptm. instead of the circus & had French fries & cheese sandwiches by Bergman. Turner worked for me.

November 10, Friday, 1944

Worked 3-11, only had 2 patients. Nothing special. Wrote letters.

November 11, Saturday, 1944

Went to Armistice Day Parade with Getz. Met Olive & gave her a note for Donnie. Ate at Seine Hq. & stopped at Donnie's office.

November 12, Sunday, 1944

Slept late. Donnie came at 11:15 & we had dinner then rode to Lava Pork, it was closed so we walked down the Champs de Elysee & then to see "The Lady in the Dark." Then to his place for supper after which Sgt. brought me back for duty at 7:00. He gave me a flashlight.

November 13, Monday, 1944

Worked split till 7 but got off early. Donnie came at 7:15. Bergman, Olive & us went to the circus then stopped in a little place & back home.

November 14, Tuesday, 1944

Donnie came at 8:00. Was at meeting having some trouble, picked up Olive & Bill at the Bullets & went to Taharen night club. Cheap floor show but we had fun. Came in late cause darn it all, start nights tomorrow, just not supposed to go with him.

November 15, Wednesday, 1944

Duffey & I both on. Slept till noon then went shopping downtown & stopped in to see Donnie. He wanted us for supper but we came back. Prepared all night for all the patients to come in hall & everywhere all the big shots were up snooping.

November 16, Thursday, 1944

Washed my hair & took a shower then went on duty 7-7. Wrote letters.

November 17, Friday, 1944

Got up at noon & met Donnie at the opera at 2:00 & we went shopping. I got doughnuts & coffee, then met him for supper with Jeep & bought perfume. Then Brady had to rush us back at 7:00.

November 18, Saturday, 1944

Went to class from 8-12 then lunch & to bed. Donnie came after us & we went down to Bullets & sat around & visited cause we couldn't go out cause they were waiting for their outfit to come in. Had a lot of fun & hated to come in & go on duty at 11pm.

November 19, Sunday, 1944

Slept all day till 5:30, then learned we were to leave nights. Cowen was up & then came back with Donnie as we were fixing our billings. Then we went to the movie, saw "Girl Cover" again. Hated to say good bye cause they were swell kids. We had fun in 2 weeks. Brady drove us around again.

November 20, Monday, 1944

Left early in morning. Stopped at Versailles.

Normandy, France

November 21, Tuesday, 1944

Struggled through another day on the train with no sleep.

November 22, Wednesday, 1944

Got here early in mud hole. Went to breakfast & rested in other kids' tents then suffered through tent of 20 in mud. Scanlan brought my Christmas package. Donnie sent & we got some mail. 3 good ones from Moe. He's having trouble again.

November 23, Thursday, 1944

Got up early but didn't have to go on duty so wrote letters etc. Before supper met with Duffey, Turner & Shier from tent of 20. Got more unusual this afternoon. Went to church & Scanlan came after. Wrote to Donnie. Good Thanksgiving dinner.

November 24, Friday, 1944

Shopped then to com. pos. to 5th. 1st day to be Bl head on Orth. – but gave baths to new pts. Rained all day as usual. Finally had a chance to talk to our T/4 Don. He came up to me at supper. Got our shoes. Stayed in. Some of the kids moved.

November 25, Saturday, 1944

Beginning to get Ward straightened. Didn't eat supper. Got 2 letters from Moe. Dressed & went to Eng. party. Turkey supper with Maj., then ditched him & danced with 2 cute 2nd Lts. all night. Had fun with him, Duffey & another Capt. Bill brought me home in a long ride on truck.

November 26, Sunday, 1944

Stayed in. Scanlan & friend came after Sheer & Turner. Brought letters from Donnie.

November 27, Monday, 1944

Worked 7-3. Took shower, washed hair then home after supper. Was in bed early. Bill & Bob came for Bud & I. We entertained them in her tent. Tompkins, Stafford & dentist came. Had good time till 1:30am.

November 28, Tuesday, 1944

Worked split till 7:00. Had meeting at 7:15. Bill & Bob met Budnist & I & took us back through mud & rain to old area. Then we went for a ride to Carentan – beautiful night.

November 29, Wednesday, 1944

Worked 7-2. Moved to 5th gen. area – tired.

November 30, Thursday, 1944

Worked split & wore combat clothes for 1st time. They looked nice. Came down & straightened tent. Boys on Ward are cute. Got mail & stayed in & straightened up.

December 1, Friday, 1944

Worked 7-3, boys in B-2 are so cute. Went to dental clinic and had x-ray. Went to U.S.O. show. "Hill Billies" & who came to sit next to us but my Sgt. Don. He's way dashing. Then Turner brought over the mail, 13 letters. Bill came down again with Bud's friend but I had her tell him I was all ready cause darn it if he showed to tell me so I could get a pass.

December 2, Saturday, 1944

Worked split 7-11 & 3-7. Got Christmas package from home & went to movie. Bill met us there. Then went to party at our tent club with Bob, Bud, everyone friendly. Danced but had terrible records.

December 3, Sunday, 1944

Worked straight till 3. Still restricted. Fire in town. Washed & wrote letters. To bed early.

December 4, Monday, 1944

Nothing special. Bill called. I wouldn't go out with him.

December 5, Tuesday, 1944

Nothing special. Went to meeting & then asked to go to night duty with Duffey, Sheer & Turner. So all 4 start nights.

December 6, Wednesday, 1944

Slept late.

December 7, Thursday, 1944

Started nights with Benjamin (night supervisor). Got in convoy of pts. Capt. Schneider got hit on head then got guards & one passed out & had to go to hospital. Went to kitchen and ate. Think I'll like it.

December 8, Friday, 1944

Duffey started & she takes ½ of hosp. & I take other. Sgt. Hill wanted to go on rounds with me. Had fun.

December 9, Saturday, 1944

Usual routine on nights, we'd go to night supper and have fun. Check census & mostly go to O.R. till time for am rounds.

December 10, Sunday, 1944

In O.R. other people would visit. We'd eat & Bowman would wash our clothes etc. Scanlan came quite often for supper.

December 11, Monday, 1944

And as often, brought letters from Donnie. All mail was good. 8 Christmas boxes, good other mail. Heard lots from Moe, almost always a few pictures enclosed. Once even 4 were enclosed.

December 12, Tuesday, 1944

Got in several convoys in period on N.D. & also got 201st personnel in at 0100 to be attached.

December 13, Wednesday, 1944

Welcoming them. One of the times we were in mess hall of the many we met Stafford, he had cute blonde Lt. with him & he finally told me the Lt. was heckling him for a date with me if he was still here when I came off nights.

December 14, Thursday, 1944

Got to be quite good friends with all the Sgts. Hill, Johnson, Virgil etc.
& they would visit us often. Several times they began feeling quite good.
Only once for Veigle.

December 15, Friday, 1944

He's cute as a bug in rug. When I went up to talk to Johnston etc. at
Proff. Service he passed out in the mud. They fixed him up & we...

December 16, Saturday, 1944

went back after rounds & he kept apologizing, so we went over the office
& he followed & wouldn't leave & finally they...

December 17, Sunday, 1944

Signed him out after about an hour and a half. The next night he came
over & all apologized & stayed a while. Then...

December 18, Monday, 1944

Came back again to the office even the next night. We had quite a fun,
nice little parties with those...

December 19, Tuesday, 1944

Kids, they're nice & cute. Had quite a few exciting incidents too. One
guard stabbed & he aimed but missed. Doubled guards & just general
excitement, even mail room horned down. Had lots of fun...

December 20, Wednesday, 1944

Also John Baumer & Mousley in O.R. Cute kids. Hill & Johnston keep
heckling us for dates, but I don't know. Several pts. died while we were
on two.

December 21, Thursday, 1944

Kids on F Block. Bob & Fiddler & Rush. Were cute & fun. Forever
planting mistletoe.

December 22, Friday, 1944

Slept all day. Got up & went to supper. Hill called & wanted me to go to the show but Duffey talked to him. We went but didn't see them. Cleaned up the tent. Lots more mail.

December 23, Saturday, 1944

Started as Bl. Hd. on H-Block. Had fun with all the kids coming over & decorating. Very cute boys. & lots of mistletoe. Cute boy finally caught one & really kissed me good on H-4 after I went to personnel to sign another paper. Johnston asked me to go to church with them Christmas Eve. Stayed in & did things in the tent in the evening.

December 24, Sunday, 1944

Worked split. Went to church. More mistletoe business. Stayed on Wd., helped make candy. Went to Sig. Cps. EM party & then to mess where we met everyone & walked home with the Sgts.

December 25, Monday, 1944
No entry.

December 26, Tuesday, 1944
No entry.

December 27, Wednesday, 1944

E.M.'s dance – 168th orch. Had super-duper time. Danced, everyone was cute. Was with Johnston mostly.

December 28, Thursday, 1944
No entry.

December 29, Friday, 1944
No entry.

December 30, Saturday, 1944

Dick Foster came after me & we went on double date to his place where they had a wonderful party for their E.M.'s. Danced with the Capt. & everyone & jitterbugged especially with his very good E.M.'s

December 31, Sunday, 1944

Went to 8th conv. Had a miserable time. Wish I hadn't gone.

January 1, Monday, 1945

Nothing special. Didn't even realize it was New Year's Day. Maybe next year will be different.

January 2, Tuesday, 1945

Nothing special.

January 3, Wednesday, 1945

Nothing special.

January 4, Thursday, 1945

Haven't heard from Moe in a while & I'm worried.

January 5, Friday, 1945

Nothing special. Moving G.I's in & out & P.W.'s in.

January 6, Saturday, 1945

Passed inspection with flying colors. The Col. & Capt. Walker said we did a fine job. Went to show in evening. Stood with Virgil. He's darling. Then to dance & danced with everyone & was cut in on lots. Had fun with MAC's especially. Good orchestra. Stern took me home.

January 7, Sunday, 1945

Worked split. Had coffee & doughnuts & cozy time in Reac. tent.

January 8, Monday, 1945

Been getting pretty much mail.

January 9, Tuesday, 1945

Nothing special. Still working hard. Wrote letters in Reac. hall. Had usual fun with MAC's at meals & in Reac. Hall.

January 10, Wednesday, 1945

Worked straight & transferred patients out & others in. Took shower then to lecture. We all wanted to go to movie and see "Till We Meet Again" but Col. wanted him to clean up papers so we went with Buzz.

January 11, Thursday, 1945

Worked split – usual day. Still sick P.W.'s stayed in wreck tent on split time.

January 12, Friday, 1945

No entry.

January 13, Saturday, 1945

No entry.

January 14, Sunday, 1945

No entry.

January 15, Monday, 1945

No entry.

January 16, Tuesday, 1945

No entry.

January 17, Wednesday, 1945
No entry.

January 18, Thursday, 1945
No entry.

January 19, Friday, 1945
No entry.

January 20, Saturday, 1945
No entry.

January 21, Sunday, 1945
No entry.

January 22, Monday, 1945
No entry.

January 23, Tuesday, 1945
No entry.

January 24, Wednesday, 1945
No entry.

January 25, Thursday, 1945
No entry.

January 26, Friday, 1945
No entry.

Carentan/Cherbourg, France

January 27, Saturday, 1945
No entry.

January 28, Sunday, 1945
No entry.

January 29, Monday, 1945
No entry.

January 30, Tuesday, 1945
No entry.

January 31, Wednesday, 1945
No entry.

February 1, Thursday, 1945
No entry.

February 2, Friday, 1945
No entry.

February 3, Saturday, 1945
Went to dance with Lawrence, Gross, Mousley etc. Capt. (dental) Buskaloo saved me from Y.M. crowd I was avoiding. He rushed me all night but got mad at the crazy M.C.'s teasing me all night too. They took me home when he left mad. Had lots of fun.

February 4, Sunday, 1945
Capt. Buskaloo asked me to go to Carentan but didn't, did go to movie in evening, went with him.

February 5, Monday, 1945
To dental clinic.

February 6, Tuesday, 1945
Officers meeting in Reac. Tent.

February 7, Wednesday, 1945
Nothing special.

February 8, Thursday, 1945
Had date with Johnston & went to town with Duffey & Austin to see "When Irish Eyes are Smiling." It was very good. Johnston is cute. Had fun time. Several nurses & G.I's were there. To dental clinic.

February 9, Friday, 1945
Veigle was down off & on & then while Johnston was sitting in the office from 6-7 he called & then I had to call him & he asked me to go to show. We saw French movie in Carentan with several other couples. Had to move several times. Had fun. Gray & Maj. Stanton were there.

February 10, Saturday, 1945
Had inspection even while they were putting in floors on block. Moved cute sweet boys on H-1 to C-1.

February 11, Sunday, 1945
Worked till noon. Was sleeping. Maj. Walker called me & coaxed me to go with a friend of his & he came down to get me & I wouldn't go. He got mad but I made a date with Johnston to go to last dance with Duffey & then she wouldn't go.

February 12, Monday, 1945
Johnston was down & wanted to know if I had a good time last night. Meeting with Capt. Walker. To dental clinic.

February 13, Tuesday, 1945

Nothing special – visited Jamie in hosp. Continued having fun with MAC officers weekly meeting in Reac. Tent.

February 14, Wednesday, 1945

Had a PM. Duffey said Johnston told her he had too much competition with Veigle & that he would start all over again after I get off nights. Met both her & Veigle grinning at me and came out the N.D. with no good letters. They're both so cute & yet so different. 2 good letters from Moe. One from Jimmy Coleman & Donnie etc. Stayed in & wrote letters. To dental clinic.

February 15, Thursday, 1945

Worked till noon. Everything smooth on block for a change. Had fun at dinner. Washed my hair & slept. Started nights again, last night in office. Called Donnie in Paris for Barb, Getz. It was swell talking to them.

February 16, Friday, 1945

No entry.

February 17, Saturday, 1945

No entry.

February 18, Sunday, 1945

No entry.

February 19, Monday, 1945

Went to utilities office for party for Duffey. Went during supper hour.

February 20, Tuesday, 1945

Duffey & kids left. Will miss her.

February 21, Wednesday, 1945
Night duty.

February 22, Thursday, 1945
Night duty routine. Not busy. Veigle visiting since Saturday.

February 23, Friday, 1945
Night duty routine.

February 24, Saturday, 1945
Veigle was in for the evening as usual & then we went to get his radio
then decided not to then he went to night supper with Bloom & Sgt.
Watering was there, drunk, funny. He came over the office then told me
about Johnston & Veigle.

February 25, Sunday, 1945
The boys cute Fidder, Thayer, Busky etc. came over & escorted us
back. They're going to the Infantry. Sgt. Wooden teased me about
blackmailing me for 5000 francs.

February 26, Monday, 1945
Night duty.

February 27, Tuesday, 1945
Veigle came over with radio. Hill was there too. Darling radio & we all
went to N.S.

February 28, Wednesday, 1945
No entry.

March 1, Thursday, 1945

Worked on A. Jamie came on in Vermilion's place. Kids on E so nice to me. Veigle brought my pay. We're supposed to be taken over.

March 2, Friday, 1945

Signed more papers in personnel & had fun with Veigle & the kids. He asked me for a date Sunday.

March 3, Saturday, 1945

Went to Carentan & shopped & took pictures with Sheer & M's. Danced with French girls. Working on V block.

March 4, Sunday, 1945

Didn't go to dance. Veigle & orchestra played.

March 5, Monday, 1945

Went to ball game on split time. Veigle came up on Ward. We went to movie in Carentan, saw Don O'Connor in "Patrick the Great."

March 6, Tuesday, 1945 – 6 mos.

Worked split till 7:00 then to ball game. Veigle came over to watch it with me. Meeting in afternoon.

March 7, Wednesday, 1945

Worked straight. Personnel (Admin.) played register. We rooted. Lawrence & I had a feud. Came home & wrote Moe.

March 8, Thursday, 1945

Closed V block. Transferred pts. Heard from Moe & Monahan again. Another ball game. Lots of promotions.

March 9, Friday, 1945

Checked Wards for Sunday's inspection. Was supposed to meet Veigle in movie but he had orchestra practice.

March 10, Saturday, 1945

Went to dance & just danced with everyone. The orchestra is super.

March 11, Sunday, 1945

Went to ball game, then on triple date with Ruffer, Cosman & kids to Carentan movie. I was with Paul Huck – nice kid. Saw "Dragon Seed."

March 12, Monday, 1945

Went to bed early but had to get up cause the ordinance fellows came up for a while.

March 13, Tuesday, 1945

Worked long & hard on V-block.

March 14, Wednesday, 1945

Worked split & Capt. Katler asked me to the dance Saturday & then the others started calling cause they had till 5:30. Washed my hair.

March 15, Thursday, 1945

Worked hard on V-block till 4:00 then watched Veigle's – good fun, ball game. Wrote letters in resc. tent & Lt. Paul Huck called & said he tried yesterday too. Had to tell him of closed dance but he's coming tomorrow night. Veigle came up on Wd. this morning, we were busy with tetanus pts.

March 16, Friday, 1945

Birthday Coke & Friendly remembered but I forgot. Started on G-block. Good ball game. Veigle called me to wish me "Happy birthday." Dressed in class A. Paul Huck came up, I gave him a piece of birthday cake & Lawrence went with friend of his & we had a good time at French show.

March 17, Saturday, 1945

Worked split then to cocktail party & steak supper followed by dance with Katler. Good time.

March 18, Sunday, 1945

Spent afternoon in ball park & took pictures. Went again in evening & then to bed.

March 19, Monday, 1945

Worked straight. To ball game. Veigle watched part with me then had to be C.Q. but made me promise to come sign paper tomorrow in personnel.

March 20, Tuesday, 1945

Worked straight & hard. Went to ball game. Johnston asked me for a date again & I took my laundry down. Had usual meeting.

March 21, Wednesday, 1945

Worked split. Got swell letter from Moe finally & now I'm happy again.

March 22, Thursday, 1945

Worked till 3:00. Johnston was down & wanted me to go out & Veigle met me at noon & wanted me to go for a walk & take picture. He called & then came down but I was afraid & he got mad. Went to ball game & then the Col. had a meeting.

March 23, Friday, 1945

PM. Went to good movie with Lawrence. Met Veigle & Selock in cake bor. Went to game. They beat supply & he called & wanted me to go out again. Told me they played every night for a while. Huck called & wanted to go Sunday.

March 24, Saturday, 1945

Worked split. Veigle is in the hosp. cause of his leg. Saw him at the game. Stayed home & got ready for tomorrow.

March 25, Sunday, 1945

Went to Mont St. Michel with gang. Tiring long ride & not too interesting but glad I saw it. Capt. Boren & Christian made it fun. Got lost & home at 7:00, they served us supper. Had date with Paul Huck & went to movie in rain in town. Truck went down bridge & down river. Got lots of mail, 3 from Moe alone.

March 26, Monday, 1945

Rained again. Worked 7-2. Nothing special. Washed hair etc.

March 27, Tuesday, 1945

Another letter from Moe. Worked till 7:00pm. Nothing in evening.

March 28, Wednesday, 1945

Worked till 3, really 5. Went to see "Keys of the Kingdom."

March 29, Thursday, 1945

Had a PM – nothing special—Went to communion. Another letter from Moe.

March 30, Friday, 1945

Was off. Slept late then dressed & Lawrence & I both tried to get kids to Cherbourg. Went to church & PX. Wrote letters & then ball game. First time I'd seen Veigle in a week & he was hurt cause I didn't go up & see him in hosp.

March 31, Saturday, 1945

Worked straight. Went to ball game & Veigle was there as usual.

MEMORNADA

Boring month. No fun taking care of P.W.'s. Moe & I are really discussing the most serious parts of our lives.

April 1, Sunday, 1945

Worked till 3. Nothing special. Went to church morning & evening. Wrote letters. Last day on G. Went into Seersuckers Easter Sunday.

April 2, Monday, 1945

Worked split. Good to be back on H again. Another sweet letter from Moe. Rained all day.

April 3, Tuesday, 1945

Had a PM. Met Veigle at cake bar after getting rations. He says his leg is to bother him all his life. Went to movie in eveing.

April 4, Wednesday, 1945

Funny, exciting game. The M.C.'s played the MAC's & knocked their socks off.

April 5, Thursday, 1945

Went to meeting. Good letters from Moe.

April 6, Friday, 1945

Left in trucks from Hq. at 0800 for 2 days at Granville. Met kids who know nurses I know at home & 3rd gen. – Helen Meyers & Esther, nice kids & we went around with them. Granville, clean, picturesque. Restful but only movies & doughnuts.

April 7, Saturday, 1945

Slept late, it was wonderful & comfortable bed. Shopped & talked with G.I.'s on blvd. Went to dance which was a flag at 10:30. Thank goodness it was ours at 10:30.

April 8, Sunday, 1945

Slept well. I heard Gross & Neff about 10 then rushed to get his Jeep back. Relief to get home after last night's 4:15 alarm. Good game, we won from 176th. Games all afternoon & evening. Then good movie.

April 9, Monday, 1945

Worked split. Johnston told me he's staying behind. I hate that. He came down to take my films to x-ray. Went to 2nd ball game after supper. Veigle & I are very cold anymore. I can't help he doesn't use any direction. Darling letter from Bob.

April 10, Tuesday, 1945

Had a PM. Had good times on duty, the kids are nice. Had my hair cut, Lawrence did it. Watched 2 games. Veigle came over then sat next to me. I guess he isn't mad anymore.

April 11, Wednesday, 1945

Nothing unusual.

April 12, Thursday, 1945

President Roosevelt died.

April 13, Friday, 1945

Good gang in our outfit. Friendly & charming.

April 14, Saturday, 1945

No entry.

April 15, Sunday, 1945

Usual games. Memorial service for president.

April 16, Monday, 1945

Usual games.

April 17, Tuesday, 1945

Ball games & usual days. Capt. Draper inspected & questioned me.

April 18, Wednesday, 1945

Had a PM. Got sun tan & then to 2 ball games. Veigle hangin around & I didn't pay any attention to him. He doesn't hold his place. Went to stage show at 180th with gang & came home with gang.

April 19, Thursday, 1945

Had day off & Lawrence & I went to Cherbourg in ambulances, each in a different one. Rode with cute infantryman L/Sgt. for 7 months & didn't know it. Ernie Pyle killed.

April 20, Friday, 1945

Everyone cheered for Johnston & his no-hit game last night with 165th at the game tonight & I got ready for him tomorrow. Washed hair & lost my pink pants coming back from shower.

April 21, Saturday, 1945

Worked till 7. Johnston came up & I gave him the whiskey & he spent the afternoon & we made a date for tomorrow night.

April 22, Sunday, 1945

We all took more time off & I went off at 3. Bohick came over & told me Johnny had tried to get in touch with me but that they all decided to make it tomorrow night.

April 23, Monday, 1945

Had a PM. We're going to take the 165th in Cherbourg. Darn. Went to ball game. 2 letters from Moe. Meeting with Capt. Walker. Johnston said he felt awful but they were having a farewell. Was talking to champ on phone & then met Johnston in post office.

April 24, Tuesday, 1945

Had a PM. Johnston called on duty and said he'd call at 5:30 in her house, then Capt. Walker was in there so I didn't wait & I tried to call him & couldn't. Went to Ball game & then to movie to see "Our Hearts Were Young and Gay" cause we made it tomorrow night.

April 25, Wednesday, 1945

Slept late – worked 1-7. Johnston was up & then stopped me on walk. Later made arrangements for Lawrence & Savage & we all met in Rode Champ & Bohick. Had fun visiting farm houses both occupied & unoccupied. He's very sweet. We got lost, very nice & not smart. He said he'd give me perfume O'Dorsey he had for me tomorrow night.

April 26, Thursday, 1945

Worked 7-3. Johnston & Blum were up. Col. Wallegora & inspecting party were here. Guess we passed. Went to game & then to meeting. Jamie was mad cause I didn't go with Johnston again cause she went with kid from motor pool.

April 27, Friday, 1945

Nothing special.

April 28, Saturday, 1945

Had P.M. Packed – Johnston called twice. Said farewell & good riddance to P.W.'s. Met Johnston & went for walk in Carentan. Got wine, he's sweet. Gave me darling bottle of Trophee D'Orsay. Asked me to get his present & said he'll be coming up to Cherbourg. Hate to leave him.

April 29, Sunday, 1945

Left early from Carentan in ambulance for Paris with Lawrence, Cosman, Ruffer & Zeigler. Got off train & to hotel about 8 – orchestra & choir. Went with 4 officers.

April 30, Monday, 1945

Had our pictures taken & went on tour at 1:00 pm. Had pictures taken. Bus broke down & Frenchmen fixed it. Fellows & officers followed us to hotel & insisted on taking us out but in evening Lawrence & I ditched them at The Folies but met & sat and went to cute air corps kids who brought us home & to coffee & doughnuts in one hour.

Arlene with Eiffel Tower behind her.

May 1, Tuesday, 1945

Met the 2 air corps kids early Jack & Lin went to QM & bought Eisenhowers & they came to hotel for lunch. Met French Lt. from the 25th & also Badger from the 3rd then we went shopping again on the metro & to Lt. Lounge . Jack bought me Lily of the Valley & then we went to Seeing base Hq. to wait for me. Kinney's Bf with Lawrence. I tried to call Moe. Then the Café de la Paix & French lady fixes my corsage, took all 3 boys to supper & then we went out in evening. Stopped in all over.

May 2, Wednesday, 1945

Left hotel early. Went to station on metro. Had trouble getting seats – 6 officers with me, 4 kids in complainant. Ruffer, Casmen & Lawrence. Had fun but married. Larry met us at station in Cherbourg. Came back to new area. Worn out.

May 3, Thursday, 1945

Had PM. Wonderful – Heavenly taking care of new G.I.'s with their teasing & lines. They saluted us all over the place due to new delinquency sheets etc. Had meeting in evening. Fixed tent. Cute & homey.

May 4, Friday, 1945

Slept late & worked 1-7. Took shower & washed hair.

May 5, Saturday, 1945

Had a PM. G.I.'s swell. Had inspection. Nothing special, didn't care to go to any parties. Stayed in & went to movie.

May 6, Sunday, 1945

Slept late. Worked 1-7. Nothing special.

May 7, Monday, 1945

Had a PM. Went to Cherbourg with Jamie. Stayed home in evening. Hills started ringing & shots fired.

May 8, Tuesday, 1945

V.E. Day! Worked only 1 ½ hours. Church bells rang all day. In evening
Champ coaxed me to go with Rodebough so I did with Champ &
Bobbick, Findley, Sexton & Sgt. & Wright. Walked to beach. It was
gorgeous. We had front row seats for fireworks & search lights. He's cute
& very nice. Got in at 0300.

May 9, Wednesday, 1945

V.E. Day. Overslept till 9:00 so the kids said to come on at 1 & take an
AM instead of a PM. Schwabenlard was up & said Johnny was with
him & tried to call me. I went to movie with Greenfield & we met him in
front of the movie. People all around.

May 10, Thursday, 1945

Worked 7-1. Johnston & Schosh were up at 0800. They stayed all night.
We were going to the E.M.'s dance till we were absolutely forbidden &
then we were going for a walk but then that was cancelled. Rody called
& asked me to go to picnic again tomorrow.

May 11, Friday, 1945

Slept late. Worked 1-3 then went off. Wrote letters & then had meeting
after supper. Met the boys down the old back road & walked to the
beach/ Had lots of fun as usual. I like Rody a lot. He told me about the
boys Hill, Johnston & all knowing about us right away.

May 12, Saturday, 1945

Worked 7-1. Had inspection & passed. Very hot in afternoon. Stafford
said Starn was going to ask me to a dance at 812th had I told them all
I was not dating our officers. Went to show. Lots of chances to go to
parties & dates galore to go to our dance but stayed in & wrote letters.
Rice told me she & Capt. Bell saw us last night & she likes Rodenbaugh
very much. I really hope he waits for me for 2 weeks & I kinda think he
will but you can't tell.

May 13, Sunday, 1945

Worked 7-1. Went on at N. hosp. at 7:00pm. Sgt. Ducksworth on nights. Stayed on A with Avery most of night.

May 14, Monday, 1945

Had meeting after ball game. NO dating of E.M.S. per order. Col. Signed pry voucher later in personnel they were all working late. Sgt. Shick told me Rodebough was up so I guess Findley told him.

May 15, Tuesday, 1945

Had an awful time sleeping. Been getting good letters from Moe. Rody called several times & then gone to switchboard his initials. He & Champ & Johnny were up & I talked to Rody on the main walk & we decided it was best I was on nights & we'd just bide our time. Veigle & Blueburn were drunk & Veigle hunted me till he found me. Got in train of G.I.'s.

May 16, Wednesday, 1945

No entry.

May 17, Thursday, 1945

Slept well & went to ball game & Veigle came over & asked about last night & talked for a while then I talked to them later in personnel. Got another train.

May 18, Friday, 1945

Nothing special.

May 19, Saturday, 1945

Got cute note from Rody & talked to Champ. Duckworth talked to me & pleaded with me not to marry Moe.

May 20, Sunday, 1945

Cute patients – Busy. Veigle drunk.

May 21, Monday, 1945

Nothing special – Veigle drunk again – followed me in the dining room. Rody couldn't get call through. Operators wouldn't let him.

May 22, Tuesday, 1945

Slept late. Hill stopped me going on duty & told me to come back he had a note. Veigle was sober for a change. Cute note with 2 from Rody. I answered it. E-block was busy.

May 23, Wednesday, 1945

Got up early & went in to see "Dear Ruth" Dorothy McGuire at 4:30. It was wonderful. Had fun coming home in cab with Maj. Stanton & other officer. Laughed until we cried. Only slept 2 hours.

May 24, Thursday, 1945

Bumped into Champ & finally all evening & then Johnny came up to meet them & let it slip about Rody's birthday so I wrote a note.

May 25, Friday, 1945

Met Rody early on D but could only talk for a second cause I was busy & people around & Anderson got sick. Once he started down the path with me & the cab met us but he dashed. Then he came up on D with Shick & they made toast & coffee for all of us & Maj. Kirtz sat & talked & liked Rody a lot. Then Findley, Johnny & Champ came after him.

May 26, Saturday, 1945

Got up for supper. We were very busy. Couple more trains – they had to put up more & more tents. Veigle came over after the dance for his lecture & I talked & talked to him on A about drinking & women. Washed my hair. Boy called & wants date – I talked to him last week.

May 27, Sunday, 1945

Slept late till 5:30. Then Bohick told me Rody was C.Q. Jean & I went to movie & saw "Cinderella Jones" & then wrote letters & got cleaned up. Rody called & explained. Officers called & coaxed for us to go to parties but had a lot to do at home.

May 28, Monday, 1945

Worked on G-block. In evening met kids & Rody & I talked & talked & he likes me so much he's afraid & so am I. He told me what Shick & all said about kissing me & he still hasn't. I can't tell him to & he's afraid I won't let him & he's also afraid of himself. I feel funny for the first time in a long time. Different than Donnie or anyone since Moe & I so want him to kiss me. I'm awfully afraid he won't call.

May 29, Tuesday, 1945

Had a PM. Some of the boys left. Nice ones left. Rody called & we made date for tomorrow night.

May 30, Wednesday, 1945

Met the kids & took pictures then we found a cute comf. fox hole & started where we left off Mon. Rody finally asked me if I wanted to get a good lunch in a hurry & oh golly do I like him. I was afraid maybe, that he would be the only thing & that I wouldn't like the way he kisses. But he makes me melt.

May 31, Thursday 1945

Nothing special.

MEMORANDA

Strange, confusing, contented month. Happier than for a very long time. I could love him I believe but I'm afraid.

June 1, Friday, 1945

Got off late. Cute patients. G.I.'s & Findley came over with a very important looking note from Rod which after all his & Hills trouble was just a cute cartoon. Met the kids & we had a sorta picnic in woods. Candy, nuts, cookies & champagne. Then I polished my nails & we talked & it rained. I really like him, he makes me melt. He says he wants the web to get tighter & stranger around the fly. It was 2:30am.

June 2, Saturday, 1945

Had a 3:00pm off. Cutly had night, they leave tomorrow. We walked to fort on Channel & met the boys & they were all so cute as usual. We had chicken sandwiches & wine. Rod brought snapshot book with him & showed me his mom & dad & home etc. Rod is darling & I could like him very much but I'm afraid. We got in at 0300 after long walk back. I hate to see those kids leave. It will be hard for Champ & Findley.

June 3, Sunday, 1945

Went to church – had split. Exhausted after last night. Have cold so to bed early.

June 4, Monday, 1945

Had split time. One of the boys gave me another darling note from Rod. He called in evening & made plans for tomorrow. To bed early.

June 5, Tuesday, 1945

Worked split. Went to G.I. show with Rice then stopped in pts. Mess to make chicken sandwiches & Dutch Holland came in & started imitating Rod "I'm certainly glad I found you out." Met Avery & we met the boys at the comp after missing them on the short cut. Danced with R.C. Had champagne. Cute place & Rod good dancer. Pretty front yard – got in at 3:00 am again.

June 6, Wednesday, 1945

Dead tired. Only one on so Capt. Wood keys & took 9-1 off. When I got there the boys were there. Champ, Findley & Rod. He stayed all night in Dutch's bed. Slept late. Then left & came back later with a note which Champ handed me for him. They're darling & pts. & corpsmen like him.

June 7, Thursday, 1945

Had PM. Then after Rod called made arrangements for Waltz to meet us & Jean said she'd go. We had meetings so we were late but we met them down the road & I just think he's darling all the time. He said he'd like to go out every night & planned on week-ends if we got married. He's cute as he can be. He stopped on Wd. & told Jamie about her promotion & she thinks he's cute. He said what I knew he would just word for word as Bob did & made me gasp—that I really should marry him cause I wouldn't even have to change my initials.

June 8, Friday, 1945

Had split time. Got 3 beautiful letters from Moe which made me really stop & think. I'm so confused I don't know which end's up. They're both too wonderful for me and I don't deserve either. Oh, how can I get so mixed up.

June 9, Saturday, 1945

Got sandwiches & met Avery then we met the boys down at the Good Deal Chateaux. Rod brought good cards & we danced & had a lot of fun. Then when they left, Shick gave Rod the key & said we could Sun. & Mon. but we're too tired. Got in at 0300.

June 10, Sunday, 1945

Slept late. Worked 1-7. Nothing doing much. New Dr. in our outfit who remembered me from 217th Gen. went to see Ray Millard in "Mystery." Rod sure does remind me of him. Sgt. Shick got orders and left already.

June 11, Monday, 1945

Had a PM. Nothing special all day. Rod called & we're going to go tomorrow night.

June 12, Tuesday, 1945

Had a PM. Made arrangements with Whaley for Jean & tonight then went to ball game & sat with Findley then Rod & Champ came up & we watched the game. Then we left & met them down the road & went to the cottage. We played cards & the boys did tricks & we danced but something was wrong between Rod & I that I couldn't put my finger on.

June 13, Wednesday, 1945

Worked 7-1. Whaley says I should go half way. Went to movies with Jean. Nice movie house talking to Findley & he says Rod is nuts about me. Can't wait till he calls Friday.

June 14, Thursday, 1945

Had another PM. Went to Cherbourg.

June 15, Friday, 1945

No entry.

June 16, Saturday, 1945

Gosh, what a mess, they tried to send me to I&E school. Staffie needed somebody in a hurry & Capt. Walk, Capt. Alphs & Capt. Draper got orders & after we all fought things were changed. Rod called at noon & wanted me to go out. I had to walk down the road to the path to meet him & met a command car with Col. & Maj. We had a swell time. He makes me melt. Got in at 0130.

June 17, Sunday, 1945

Slept late till noon & worked 1-7. Met Rod down at the church after meeting patients galore. Hate to walk down that road alone. We talked & had·fun but we're still all mixed up.

June 18, Monday, 1945

Had PM. Stayed in to get ready.

June 19, Tuesday, 1945

Had PM. Went with Gross to meet Rod & he had to look for her T/5. We had fun just talking & stuff. He told me how much he's going to miss me & I know I'll miss him. He's going to try to go to Paris & meet me there Sunday. T/4 Whaley & Pt. Robert Day called me to say good bye. Gross took the message.

June 20, Wednesday, 1945

Left 196th Cherbourg about 0730 with Jamie, Mel, Hauser & McKinney rode with Maj. Connely & Capt. Huber. Had fun. Arrived in Paris & finally got set up at "Etats Unis" Hotel. Went to Olympia & saw good stage show. Then Rainbow Room for coffee & doughnuts where we met sailors who took us to G.I. nightclub. They wouldn't let us in so we went to Pigalle. Finally got in after walking home & washed my hair.

June 21, Thursday, 1945·

Slept late then went to PX & off. Mess & QM. Then finally met at station for a 2 hour ride. Left at 1700.

June 22, Friday, 1945

Got in at 1700. Met Beaucomp girls from 3rd Gen'l and all over. Jamie, Cromley, Graner & all were on our train. Got off at Marseille. Got registered & set up at hotel with Jamie & Moe & Mel next door. Met Lawrence & the kids & friend of Lawrence wanted date to sit at General's table but didn't get to nor want to.

June 23, Saturday, 1945

Went to PX & Pierce met me there, then walked me back & we went to Eden Roc. Saw Dorothy McGuire & cast of "Dear Ruth" in wash room & Bob drove us home & waited while I changed & then drove us to town & we went to PX, window shopped & dinner.

June 24, Sunday, 1945

Slept in & then to beach. Went to Provence all 4 of us & met Norm, Greg & Arnie. Had fun – good dancers. Bob called earlier & wanted me to go with the Col. but I wouldn't.

June 25, Monday, 1945

Went to beach & then we got home & dressed. Norm came up at 2:00. I wouldn't go with him but made plans for him to get Jamie a date & we all 4 went to do the town from the Martinez to Hotel Normandy. Had fun with cute air corps Jetersburg at Normandy who had to leave next morning. He came down to the truck even to see us off.

June 26, Tuesday, 1945

Had fun on beach in Pedals & stuff. Borrowed $20 from air corp. off. who left & we have his money. Went down to see "Dear Ruth." Came back to Provencal & met Gregg & Norm. They were drunk so I wouldn't stay. Norm called & I wouldn't go with him.

June 27, Wednesday, 1945

Had breakfast & then got ready & went to Eden Roc for lunch, we 4 had fun. It was windy & the water was rough. Couldn't go in again but had fun talking to everyone, especially the Capt who reminded me of Hebel. In evening, we went up Provencal to get reservations for Monte Carlo and danced with Marine 25 C. Maj. Very cute, fun & good dancer. After Moe ditched the Col. we went downtown & met Arnie, Gregg & Norm while getting on truck. He bought me carriage & we did the town.

June 28, Thursday, 1945

Slept in. Went to beach in afternoon. Went to PX with Mel & met kids from Ashford. Went for ride & had fun. Came back & there was Norm. I got hauled out from the kids for snubbing Norm, so ended up making date with him Mel, Gregg – Mac, Arnie & we did the town again. Supper at the Martinez, Lorina & Normandy hotel. Saw the Maj. with French girl. Danced with air corps kids again at the Normandy. Cute & good dancer.

June 29, Friday, 1945

Slept in & then dinner before going to beach. Spent the afternoon there but water rough. Norm called but I wouldn't go with him. Told him we 4 were going stag which we did but first thing off the hat we met him there & I tried to spurn him & ended up with another good dancer. He was mad at me for a while but later we all exchanged dances.

June 30, Saturday, 1945

Awakened & ate breakfast at Juan-les-Pino & on our way at 0415, train left at 0530. Read & slept all the way to Paris from Cannes. Riviera beautiful.

MEMORANDA

Riviera: If only I could have been with Moe there & Rod in Paris. I'm sure it would have helped.

July 1, Sunday, 1945

Slept late & through dinner after getting in Paris at 0500 & then to a mess from station & to our old hotel from last week. Got up & went to Cos. off. Mess then to look for note from Rod or Moe at base & Rainbow Room then to movie & back in metro to R.C. for coffee & doughnuts after a little song fest started back to hotel. Then we acted as a refuge to protect cute little air corps officers from French girls.

July 2, Monday, 1945

Had breakfast at Casual officer's mess. Nice. Train ride home & got in early. Got mail & supper. Lots of mail from Moe & he thinks I'm really serious about Rod but sweet mail & a picture. Stayed in and wrote Moe.

July 3, Tuesday, 1945

Back to G-block. Good to see everyone again even if it is a let down. Whaley told me Rod missed me & wants to go out tonight. I waited all night & he didn't call again. The line was busy tho! Wrote letters. Got sandwiches at the club & got a lot done.

July 4, Wednesday, 1945

Worked straight. Sgt. Duckworth was down & arguing for at least 2 hours.

July 5, Thursday, 1945

Had a PM. Beaucoup mail & another from Moe. Findley brought me one from Rod explaining about being in Germany for a week. Went to 280 Sta. with Moe, Mel & Jamie & saw "Wilson."

July 6, Friday, 1945

Worked split. Nice cute patients. Stayed in & wrote letters. Got pretty ring from one taken from Rhine area.

July 7, Saturday, 1945

Nothing special. Went to movie.

July 8, Sunday, 1945

Slept in. Had an AM. Cute patients, Brought field glasses from P1. Stayed in in evening instead of going to Stockade party. Rod called about 9:30pm. He's back from Germany.

July 9, Monday, 1945

Had a 9-1 off. Washed my hair. Rod called me about 11am from the Ward. He was up there. Came up with records. Met him in evening at Little Old Mom's House. I wore my blue Plaz dress & Rod went nuts about it. I showed him pictures.

July 10, Tuesday, 1945

Had a 11-3 off. Rained all day. Had fun with patients. Went to hear band in evening. They played symphony then we stayed for movie "Between 2 Girls."

July 11, Wednesday, 1945

Had a PM. Shipment left for home again. Billy among them, he took a note home for me. Wrote letters. Rod called, said he sent a note & he's leaving the 17th.

July 12, Thursday, 1945

T/4 Whaley went up Hq. for me & got a sweet kinda desperate letter from Rod from Hill for me. Went with Gross, met the fellows. We talked & told jokes & had a wonderful time. He said in another month or lots less if he stayed we'd be married.

July 13, Friday, 1945

Had 3 off. Rod called at 7:00pm & they have to work late getting ready for Thursday.

July 14, Saturday, 1945

Had a 11-3 off. Had Maj. here to inspect. Rod phoned & said he'd be late. He had picture & his name & address & stuff for me. We had fun sitting under protective covering in pouring down rain until it fell apart. Rod dashed after the Jeep in motor pool & came & picked me up & we rode down the road a piece. He had to come back at 0100 to take an officer home from the dance.

July 15, Sunday, 1945

Had PM. Was going on picnic with Rod, Findley, Champ but it rained & Rod didn't get in till 0430 last night cause he had to wait. Patients sent me flowers from this walk.

July 16, Monday, 1945

Took a PM but Rod couldn't make it cause they had a meeting till 9:30pm. I'm going to miss him.

July 17, Tuesday, 1945

Had our old usual place. He's darling. Came in early as he couldn't get
picked up by P's again.

July 18, Wednesday, 1945

Had a PM. Rod called at 2:30 & said he couldn't came in afternoon but
would call at 5:30 & he's sure to be out tonight. He was brought off. I
wore my blue suit he loves. I really think he loves me. We didn't say
good bye but good night & he wanted to keep on going but I get stuck in,
let him read letter Moe sent to Ruth May.

July 19, Thursday, 1945

Rod left this morning for La Houre & the states. Oh if only I could have
gone too. Worked 9-1 off. Was C.Q. after meeting. Wrote letters. Got
one from Moe.

July 20, Friday, 1945

Went to French show at theater. It was very good.

July 21, Saturday, 1945

Jean & Jamie came.

July 22, Sunday, 1945

Worked 7-3. Had fight with Stafford at supper table over E.M.'s. Went
to movie in evening.

July 23, Monday, 1945

Had PM. Went to Cherbourg with Jamie & Jean & picked up our
shoes & then had ice cream. Came back just in time for Gross wedding.
Went to G.I. variety show & they had wonderful jam session. Benny
Goodman's piano played. We stayed & I danced on stage with Dutch &
trumpet played.

July 24, Tuesday, 1945

Went to show. Didn't go on duty except 7-9. Wrote letters.

July 25, Wednesday, 1945
Went to show – Olsen & Johnson to club.

July 26, Thursday, 1945
Meeting cancelled. Nothing special.

July 27, Friday, 1945
Nothing special.

July 28, Saturday, 1945
Went to show.

July 29, Sunday, 1945
Had a PM. Moe called me long distance from Reins. He's going straight to JB2. I went to Capt. Walker in afternoon & coaxed for leave. Saw "Valley of Decision" in evening.

July 30, Monday, 1945
Sweating out call from Moe.

July 31, Tuesday, 1945
Had an AM. Called Capt. Mahoney for permission to call Reins. Finally got through & left message. I was coming Thurs. or Fri. Then left note in Capt. Walker's bed that I wanted a pass Thursday.

MEMORNADA
Going to see Moe. I'm sure of it.

August 1, Wednesday, 1945
Had an AM. Capt. Walker said I could go on pass tomorrow – 60 hour. Moe called at 7pm & Jamie & all were looking for me & they called land speaker. I was in R.C. looking for white shoe polish. Capt. Walker cute giving me advice.

August 2, Thursday, 1945

Started out early with Ursula & we had pleasant company, 2 Lts. & Capt. & English Maj. Finally bulleted Normandy when Moe & Dan (of all people) grabbed me. I cleaned up & we had supper in Attic, a beautiful club like Mess. & they played "Symphony." Then we went to French place & ate again then he rode us to see town. Danced to symphony at Allies Off. Club & then to Montmartre with Leshions. Interesting. Danced with everyone including French Morrocan & back.

August 3, Friday, 1945

Went back to hotel on 1st metro. I slept & got cleaned up & then Moe came after me & we went after Dan & had lunch. Took pictures, then went for walk & talked & talked. He really likes me. Met Capt. Levine & drank champagne at Independence Club. Had supper again & then to my hotel to get this junk & I went to station to see them off. They coaxed & I went to Chalous & rode truck to Reines & then stayed at 128th Gen'l, about 5am.

August 4, Saturday, 1945

Slept till 10:00. Then nurse called me & hitched ride to town & Officers Club. Went to dinner with Para. Lt. – 2 weddings. Officers nice. Finally, Moe managed to get in. We had nice talk & he really wants to marry me I know. Walked around town & ate in Off. Mess. He put me on train & I felt awful saying good bye. He was so cute. Back at hotel, met lots of kids but talked to Wachsmith & her brother. Wrote letter to Moe.

August 5, Sunday, 1945

Wachsmith & Bud went to church & then we had coffee & doughnuts & to station. Had nice trip back. Met lots of our kids. Went to show & everyone thought I'd be married.

August 6, Monday, 1945

Had an AM. Went to ball game & then U.S.O. show.

August 7, Tuesday, 1945

G-block closed. No patients PM. Nothing special. Wrote letters.

August 8, Wednesday, 1945

Slept in. Went to work on D-block. Crazy kids. Went to show in evening.

August 9, Thursday, 1945

Worked 7-1. Nothing special. Went to movie on Living in the Jungle.

August 10, Friday, 1945

Nothing special.

August 11, Saturday, 1945

Nothing special.

August 12, Sunday, 1945

Nothings special. Still haven't heard from Rod or Moe.

August 13, Monday, 1945

Nothing special. Like D-block.

August 14, Tuesday, 1945

Had AM on D-block. Went to see crazy movie & nice song fest. Went to bed about 0100 when the kids called me at 0115 shouting "The wars over." We turned on radio & they played the national anthem. Wrote letters & then we all dressed in slacks & went up the club which still didn't have too much life. So we snuck over the E.M. Day room & Capt. Walker, Capt. Mahoney & all ended up there drinking beer & kissing one another & had lots and lots of fun just being with those swell kids even if lots of them were smoochers.

August 15, Wednesday, 1945

Had PM. Worked on Off. Wd. I-block. Dead tired from no sleep. Findley, Hill, Duck & all the boys were up as usual. All still feeling good. It's so wonderful & yet hard to comprehend after all these years.

August 16, Thursday, 1945

Had PM. Was going to town but it looked like rain. Findley grabbed me & told me good news of our orders that we leave the 5th. If only they don't change.

August 17, Friday, 1945

Worked split. Back over on G. Got in patients. Stayed in. Nothing special.

August 18, Saturday, 1945
No entry.

August 19, Sunday, 1945
No entry.

August 20, Monday, 1945
No entry.

August 21, Tuesday, 1945
No entry.

August 22, Wednesday, 1945
No entry.

August 23, Thursday, 1945
No entry.

August 24, Friday, 1945
No entry.

August 25, Saturday, 1945
No entry.

August 26, Sunday, 1945
No entry.

August 27, Monday, 1945
Finally got mail from Moe. Jamie brought them to me at supper time.

August 28, Tuesday, 1945
Split time. Good & cute patients. Went to see "Hollywood Canteen" & it split & stopped right in the middle. Went to club & ate some awful stuff at club.

August 29, Wednesday, 1945
Had PM. Jamie, Artie Weisnuski, De Rosa & all others on phone, crazy as they called several times. Went to Biology. Interesting class with cute lab kids. Capt. Belnap, Capt. Walker & Maj. Went to Brussels for promotion in Jeep. Rode to town with Jamie & all Inf. Officers in weapons carrier. Went shopping. Took pictures. Met cute patients, paratroopers in B.C. Club & took more pictures. Then ride back on truck again. Went to see "Junior Miss."

August 30, Thursday, 1945
No entry.

August 31, Friday, 1945
Come on nights on G-block. Really going to enjoy it, good bunch of boys.

September 1, Saturday, 1945
No entry.

September 2, Sunday, 1945
No entry.

September 3, Monday, 1945

No entry.

September 4, Tuesday, 1945

Finally got letter from Rod. Got more pictures for me. Boys stayed up till 0400 & wouldn't go to bed but they're fun & cute.

September 5, Wednesday, 1945

Nights. The boys all getting ready for tomorrow. Pressed clothes for some. 2 of the boys stayed up late & air corps kid. Nice & fun. Got everyone up at 0530. Such a sadness saying good bye.

September 6, Thursday, 1945

Started on F. Stockade. Wrote letters. Got up at noon & went down to see "Frances Slanger" with Cosman. Hill helped us get pass on ship. Conroy walked me off duty after I said good bye to everyone. Swell, super bunch of kids.

September 7, Friday, 1945

Working on F-block. Nights. Stockade patients only.

September 8, Saturday, 1945

Working on A. Busy but lots of fun with Beaty & McClain.

September 9, Sunday, 1945

Have fun on A – nights.

September 10, Monday, 1945

Decided to break with Moe.

September 11, Tuesday, 1945

It's best with so many differences for both of us to break up. I wrote nice letter to him.

September 12, Wednesday, 1945

Came off nights. Went to movie. Going to work on Isol. of all places.

Cherbourg Movie theater.

September 13, Thursday, 1945

Working Isol. Went to training film.

September 14, Friday, 1945

Still working Isol., don't especially like it but they're all nice. Capt. Belknap, Jamie, Pedigo, Joey & Artie & Sonala saw "A Song to Remember" movie.

September 15, Saturday, 1945

Working on Isol. Gave T.B.'s & all both. Then Donnie said F. would be busy. Worked 12 hours but like it much better almost all Orth.

September 16, Sunday, 1945

Worked split. To movie in evening, "Blondie" & song fest.

September 17, Monday, 1945

Had 3 off. Stayed in & to bed early. Tried to get Luger for Capt. Belkings. He came down & looked them over.

September 18, Tuesday, 1945

Worked split. Then had meeting & Capt. Walker said we'd be going soon. Went to movie in evening. Letters from mom & she said Lt. Dryer called at home.

September 19, Wednesday, 1945

Had 3 off. Got letter from Champ & Bohick. Findley & Dutch were down & we exchanged addresses. They told me about Johnston & wanted me to go out tonight again. He's coming up but I stayed in, washed & got things ready etc.

September 20, Thursday, 1945

Had PM. Played ping pong in club & went to training film & got ready & packed for tomorrow.

September 21, Friday, 1945

Left in morning from Cherbourg with Jane, Mullen, Goldberg & other & had to waste time in Paris. Went to movie & then got in boot train. We had to split up & I got good break, in with nice Cols. & 2 nice air corps boys. Had fun but didn't sleep much or at all. Couldn't relax neither could blonde air corps boy.

September 22, Saturday, 1945

Got off train & then onto ship. "Isle of Guernsey." Met blonde air corps boys & lots others. Roughest day in 20 years – Equarcha. Bath E.M.'s & officers a like were swell, all sick. I held out for so long then broke record & was so very sick. Got to Haven & had tea on train after processing & to England & Billing. Went to bed at 7:30pm.

September 23, Sunday, 1945

Slept late then had waffles for breakfast. Went to Mess. with kids & then back for dinner. Went to Rainbow Room & met cute boy from ship. We all went on R.C. tour & back to get cleaned up & then to office's Mess & then on bus to Scala. Play in R.C. "Boy Meets Girl" & then to underground back. Met Rosie Kramer.

September 24, Monday, 1945

After dinner Jean, Mullaly & I did business of day. Got tickets, Q.M. etc., some shopping & then back again. After supper went to see movie about English army hospital.

September 25, Tuesday, 1945

Got up early & went to see "Changing of the Guard at Buckingham." Wonderful band, bag pipes & show march. Col. Cole, elderly Englishman took us around & to his club for a drink. He was very sweet. Shopped in afternoon & in evening saw "Big Boy," musical comedy.

September 26, Wednesday, 1945

Went to Madame Tussaud's wax museum after dinner. Then to Rainbow Corner on Piccadilly Circus & had sundaes. Home to clean up & then to "The Years Between." Very good. Walked home.

September 27, Thursday, 1945

To Edinburg by long train. Arrived about 6:30. Had supper. Registered. All stay at American Service Club where G.I. & Off. all stay. Went for walk. Saw castle lit up & dancing. Went to stage show. Back at R.C. Danced & had cake. Got asked to go on date with Lt.

September 28, Friday, 1945

Got up in town to go on walking tour. Went with the Lt. After dinner shopped & had picture taken in kilts like Edinburgh.

September 29, Saturday, 1945

Liked Edinburgh very much. Everyone friendly. G.I.'s all alike. Very
picturesque & excitement all living R.C. building together. Left last
night on 7:50 train. Didn't have chance to say good bye to Lt. Dozed on
train. League of Nations slept all morning. In afternoon walked & visited
penny arcade. In evening saw "Gay Rosalinda."

September 30, Sunday, 1945

While kids went to church I went to see about plane reservations. No
good. After dinner Col. Cole took us to Windsor & Eton & had tea. After
supper went to visit Rosie & Mary.

MEMORANDA

Feel much better than last year this time cause I know I'm going back.

October 1, Monday, 1945

Went to line for plane reservation from 11:30 to 3:30 & then no trips
booked cause of cancellation. Went to PX & met Rosie. Walked home.
Went to movie in evening & then to R.C. to eat.

October 2, Tuesday, 1945

Went shopping & was going to try to get on list for plane but too long.
Met Rosie in PX. Went to see "A Night in Venice" in evening. Met 2
officers from last night in Q.M. & one of them at snack bar after play.
They were funny.

October 3, Wednesday, 1945

Went down to traffic office to sweat a plane ride after breakfast & getting
money changed. Had fun & break. They let all 3 of us Jamie, Mallaly &
I on same flight. Met Pursell & others on bus to field. It was wonderful
& beautiful flying from London to Paris.

October 4, Thursday, 1945

Had breakfast at Cos. Off. Mess after staying all night at Etats Unis. Then to train. Met Sgt. Harkin on train, nice Inf. Lt. Had gobs of mail & went to movie. Another from Rod. He still wants me to come home pronto. Kinda nice to be back.

October 5, Friday, 1945

Went to B-blocks 3 & 4. Nice patients. Kinda nice to be back. Jean came back tonight & we all went to movie.

October 6, Saturday, 1945

Worked split on E-block. Like it very much even with Simpson. The Sgts. who work there are swell & the patients can't be beat. Really had fun with them. Washed my hair in evening.

October 7, Sunday, 1945

Had PM & went to football game in truck to Tourville. Had simply super time. After supper met nice officer who wanted to play ping pong & checkers & beat him in first game. Went to show.

October 8, Monday, 1945

Worked split. Cute patient from yesterday's game is in bed on 11 with cold. Cute sweet patients. All of them.

October 9, Tuesday, 1945

Straight time. Fun with patients. Hill M/Sgt. is going home.

October 10, Wednesday, 1945

Worked straight. Saw "Christmas in Connecticut" again. Another letter from Rod.

October 11, Thursday, 1945

Worked split. Have darling patients. Got letters from Moe with pictures. Was C.Q.

October 12, Friday, 1945

Had a PM. Dashed to personnel, signed voucher & took their picture then Hanson too Cassidy, Avery & I to Lt. McGuire for football game. He wants me to go for a ride in command car with him. Collected gobs of patches from my patients. In evening saw Abbott & Costello.

October 13, Saturday, 1945

Had a 3 off. Had fun with all pats. As usual but mostly all the cute kids. E-4 doing tricks. Bought perfume from trooper's friend. I went to ball game – Pts. Vs Det & then showed the boy's in the tricks of missionaries & cannibals. Had another letter from Rod. He's really anxious for me to come home.

October 14, Sunday, 1945

Had PM. Went to football game after closing of port in Cherbourg. To movie in evening.

October 15, Monday, 1945

Worked 7-3. Had fun with pts. & corps men. Like E a lot. Got 5 letters. Cute one again from Bobick with pictures & one from Rod, he's a Sgt. To movie & then played ping pong.

October 16, Tuesday, 1945

Had 3 off. Got note from cute kid on E-11. Football game called off. Stayed home.

October 17, Wednesday, 1945

Had split time. Shipping list came out. Went to see "Here Come the Waves" Bing Crosby.

October 18, Thursday, 1945

Had 7-3. Patients were supposed to leave tomorrow, were awfully cute today. Cute pt. in E-11 insists he's writing letter to me. Sgt. in the E-4 walked off duty with me & really got mad when I wouldn't go out with him tonight. Would like to but there really is nothing to do. Went to Central Supply & cut my hair. Whaley was there.

October 19, Friday, 1945

Had 7-3. In evening went to show. Several of the new officers sat next to us. Wachsmith & kids got orders & thought surely I'd go. Played ping pong.

October 20, Saturday, 1945

Had PM. Went to football game with pts. Hillenbrand kept asking me to go to game but didn't get with him. Went to office for coffee & doughnuts at RC in Cherbourg.

October 21, Sunday, 1945

Had AM. Slept till 11am. First day of rain for long time. Pts. got money & physical at 7pm, said good bye to the boys. Wonderful bunch of pts. Hate to see them leave. Went to see "Out of This World." Another letter from Moe with more pictures.

October 22, Monday, 1945

Pts. Left at 0800 or so. Hated to see them leave. Went to breakfast with Gross at 0800 for eggs cause we were late. T/4 Eddy gave me quite a letter from Hillenbrand. Cleaned up till 3 or so. Stayed up at club & played ping pong & listened to radio. Took shower & stayed home.

October 23, Tuesday, 1945

Worked on E. again. Cleaning up. Answered Hillenbrand's letter. After meeting met truck outside, rode in truck with boys, mostly Sgts.

October 24, Wednesday, 1945

Slept in. Glad cause it was rainy & windy. Didn't do anything on duty. Went to PX, etc. Went off duty early. The kids all told me Johnston was up & wanted to see me. Then he told Findley to tell me he'd call at 9. I went to movie. Johnston called me at 11. He's leaving for Cincy in morning.

October 25, Thursday, 1945

Had PM. Offered to work on B but Capt. Walker sent me back to E. At noon Capt. Walker came after me & said I should pack, I'd be leaving soon. Jean's in hospital. Visited her a while. Then went to show and then home.

October 26, Friday, 1945

Had PM. Went to Signal Corps cable outfit with Mullaly & Jamie. Sgt. came after us. Had good steak supper & they showed us around & then we played ping pong – doubles. Had fun. Then danced to German band.

October 27, Saturday, 1945

Had AM. Nice boys on C. III & IV with Harris & I gave all influenza shots to whole block. Letter from Hebel saying he's "going home." Boys from E got pictures for me from Club. Capt. Walker visited. We went to party for Capt. Bell's farewell so we went to movie & then to club. We had a few dances. MAC officer poured out his heart about how much he liked me.

October 28, Sunday, 1945

Had a PM. Nothing unusual happened. Packed box for home. In evening went to see "Music for Millions." Wonderful but brought back memories of Bob & I was terribly blue.

October 29, Monday, 1945

Had PM. Christ asked us to go to Eng. EM's dance so Avery, Gross, McIntyre & I went mostly all from 1st armory. Gobs of fun. Cute kids who really rushed us. P.W. band Sgt. really had a crush on me & insisted I go to birthday party in tent. They called Capt. Walker to get permission to stay late but she wouldn't let us. We are going home & really appreciate everything.

October 30, Tuesday, 1945

Had AM. Washed my hair. Went to movie.

October 31, Wednesday, 1945

Got 6 letters, one from Rod & Moe. Had PM. Boys called from sig. corps dance. Fri. was CQ.

November 1, Thursday, 1945

Had AM. Slept till 11. Patients left this morning. Nothing to do on duty. Met T/4 Dickson several times. Went to movie "Roadside Manner." Had fun with Maj. Belkins later.

November 2, Friday, 1945

Had a PM. Harry Graft is back. Didn't go to E.M. dance. Had good steak supper & ice cream. Played ping pong. In evening saw "Bewitched." Good movie.

November 3, Saturday, 1945

Had an AM. Slept till 11:30. In afternoon wrote 2 long letters, one to Duffey & one to Rosemary. Nothing to do. 6 patients NP. Enjoy working with Stegman & fun with the boys.

November 4, Sunday, 1945

Had an AM. The boys from Eng. called this afternoon & I had to be rude cause Capt. Walker & all were in Gen. house. Later Brown called for one of the other boys. We talked and I apologized.

November 5, Monday, 1945

Had AM. Sgt. Brown met us at theater. 9 of us went. I sat in front with Brown & was with him mostly along with the gang of others.

November 6, Tuesday, 1945

Slept till noon. Mandy called for Sgt. Brown & said he wasn't able to call but would tomorrow night. Had day off. Capt. Walker said we'd leave the 20th. Went to movie.

November 7, Wednesday, 1945

No entry.

November 8, Thursday, 1945

Washed my hair.

November 9, Friday, 1945

Had PM. Packed box & got a few more things ready. No movie.

November 10, Saturday, 1945

Had an AM. Nothing special.

November 11, Sunday, 1945

Had PM. Went to church with Carpenter & Jack Ward. Read in afternoon. Then saw movie.

November 12, Monday, 1945

Got orders for 170th. Had an AM. Worked till 7. Then went to the party. Brownie was cuter than ever, funny, only got drunk right before we left & we had a time with him going home in Jeep.

November 13, Tuesday, 1945

Slept till noon. Packed, went to PX. Cleared post. Brownie came after Christ & I. Went to little café & then to their place. Brownie gave me his picture.

November 14, Wednesday, 1945

Started out early in ambulance & had an awful time.

November 15, Thursday, 1945

Slept late & after dinner, Wachsmith busted in on us & took me over to their area & saw Gross & all the others, came back & wrote letters in the club.

November 16, Friday, 1945

Got up & went to breakfast then in trucks to get processed. After dinner turned in money & did baggage ships & after supper went down to R.C. club with McDonney & Smittie. Some fellow Lt. Inf. wanted us to go to club with him but he was high & we met Zimmerman & another 1/Sgt. & we stayed with them & they walked us home. Went for ice cream with Smittie in afternoon.

November 17, Saturday, 1945

Donnie's here to go home with us & Christi's boyfriend & friend took Smittie & I to post party & we didn't have a good time so we left after the food & went home.

November 18, Sunday, 1945

Went for walk & took pictures. Had ice cream etc. Met Wagner & arranged to meet them at RC in evening & then they walked us home.

November 19, Monday, 1945

Moe, Smittie & I hitched a ride to La Home & went to Bill Young's place. Jamie stayed for supper & then went to rec. G.I. show. They had coffee & doughnuts.

November 20, Tuesday, 1945

Went to PX & then to get ice cream with Wagner. Fun. Then after supper the boys took us to the movies, the 6 of us went to 166th. Saw Judy Garland.

November 21, Wednesday, 1945

Met the fellows for ice cream & evening went to party in club for a while.

November 22, Thursday, 1945

The boys came after us at 11:00 & we messed around up in their office then to Thanksgiving dinner with 8 of them. After dinner went to football game. Rode in Jeep with cute little driver & Capt. & Lt. then met others. Good seats next to band.

November 23, Friday, 1945

Slept late. In afternoon went to see "You've Had It" stage show. That boy we met at spec. service put on with MOC & Smittie. Capt. Turner is here & going with the 170th. Stayed home & washed hair.

November 24, Saturday, 1945

Had meeting at 1:00 to go to "20 Grand" & Mac & I met the boys for ice cream & then coffee & doughnuts. Then we went to visit Langley & then to show & when we got back had a reunion & walked Smittie, Vaughn & Findley. Ducksworth was CQ. We picked up Wagner & went to RC. Had quite a reunion. Awfully good to see them.

November 25, Sunday, 1945

Got ice cream with the fellows & in evening they took us to show. Then had coffee & dougnuts & said good bye & thanked them for making arrangements.

November 26, Monday, 1945

Got up early & got ready. Left Phillip Morris at 2:00pm on trailer trucks & got loaded in to West Point about 4:00pm. Crowded & nothing much to do so went to bed early. 2 meals a day.

November 27, Tuesday, 1945

I'm group leader of our states & had to go to meeting. Then practiced boat drill. Went up on deck & saw the Vulcania pull into La Hore, the ship our boys are going on. Pretty sunset. Sat in lobby till movie & then they had an orchestra.

November 28, Wednesday, 1945

Listened to Navy bands on deck & bought gifts in PX & got tickets for show but didn't go. Sat in lounge with kids & read.

November 29, Thursday, 1945

Enjoyable day in lounge, on deck & playing cards – Hearts with Bess, Miller & English officers.

November 30, Friday, 1945

Really rough day. Managed to take a few pictures on deck but almost blown off – not sick so far.

December 1, Saturday, 1945

Very rough. Tail end of hurricane. Got books from library & read in lounge. In evening, we went to see movie. Heard Army – Navy game on deck. Army won.

December 2, Sunday, 1945

Went to church in movie hall. Enjoyed orchestra music. Thrilling.

Boston/Cincinnati

December 3, Monday, 1945

Got up & packed. Stayed on deck till we pulled in Boston Harbor at 1000. Debarked about noon. U.S. Train to Camp Miles Standish. Nice welcome. Comp, barracks & got cleaned up. Buses took us to chow. Wonderful steak supper. Called home & talked to Mom & Daddy. Wonderful. They're happy & so am I. They said I have mail.

December 4, Tuesday, 1945

Left Myles Standish at 9:00 & had long drawn out trip to Ft. Dix through Mass., R.I., Conn., N.Y. & then Dix at about 7:30pm. Finally got in barracks in Area 11. Living with Bass in one room. Then went to Mess. Hall, a block away & stopped in PX. Bought suitcase & a lot of stuff despite an officer, Lt. & friend following me around coaxing me to go out. Washed hair finally & got cleaned up.

December 5, Wednesday, 1945

Got up early & after breakfast filled out forms in hall for liaison officer then got N.J. physical & went to PX again after dinner packed suitcase & fixed stuff for express. Then sweated out orders – finally got settled at Separations with Knight from Knox.

December 6, Thursday, 1945

Slept late & started processing at 12:30. Filled in papers galore. Then rode to Off. Club with friend of Baé. Called home again. Then had nice supper. After supper wrote letter to Mac, Rod then had sundae and sandwich at snack bar & talked to Lt. Bess.

December 7, Friday, 1945

No entry.

December 8, Saturday, 1945

Had physical & got paid. Left Ft. Dix at 1100 & got train in Trenton for N.Y. Helped Bess, Miller get set up at New Yorker. Met Johnny on street then got 4:45 train. Met 3 swell people including cute Irishman who paid for my dinner then invited us to his compartment for a drink. Had fun.

December 9, Sunday, 1945

Didn't sleep much at all & got to Cincinnati 3 hours late, 11:20 instead of
8:20. Mom, Daddy, Ruthie May met me. Then had dinner & read mail.
Lots of it including cute letter from Sgt. Brown. Went visiting around
then Alma, Gramma & Aunt Geneva came over.

Last note I received from my grandma:

Dear Johnny,

I didn't forget your birthday because I remember the day and moment very well! You were wonderful the moment you were born and you still are now. My friends and relatives can all tell you the blessing you were and are to me - you never let me down and I love you dearly!

Grandma "absent minded but intelligent" Windhorst

My sisters wedding, June 23, 2001

Thank you, Grandma, for leaving me this amazing gift to share with our family. I hope I didn't let you down.

Made in the USA
Monee, IL
22 November 2019